SYSTEMIC INJUSTICE:

Torture, "Disappearance," and Extrajudicial Execution in Mexico

Human Rights Watch
New York · Washington · London · Brussels

Copyright © January 1999 by Human Rights Watch.
All rights reserved.
Printed in the United States of America.

ISBN #1-56432-198-3
Library of Congress Catalog Card Number: 98-83148

Addresses for Human Rights Watch
350 Fifth Avenue, 34th Floor, New York, NY 10118-3299
Tel: (212) 290-4700, Fax: (212) 736-1300, E-mail: hrwnyc@hrw.org

1522 K Street, N.W., #910, Washington, DC 20005-1202
Tel: (202) 371-6592, Fax: (202) 371-0124, E-mail: hrwdc@hrw.org

33 Islington High Street, N1 9LH London, UK
Tel: (171) 713-1995, Fax: (171) 713-1800, E-mail: hrwatchuk@gn.apc.org

15 Rue Van Campenhout, 1000 Brussels, Belgium
Tel: (2) 732-2009, Fax: (2) 732-0471, E-mail:hrwatcheu@skynet.be

Web Site Address: http://www.hrw.org

Listserv address: To subscribe to the list, send an e-mail message to majordomo@igc.apc.org with "subscribe hrw-news" in the body of the message (leave the subject line blank).

Human Rights Watch is dedicated to
protecting the human rights of people around the world.

We stand with victims and activists to prevent
discrimination, to uphold political freedom, to protect people from inhumane
conduct in wartime, and to bring offenders to justice.

We investigate and expose
human rights violations and hold abusers accountable.

We challenge governments and those holding power to end abusive practices
and respect international human rights law.

We enlist the public and the international community
to support the cause of human rights for all.

HUMAN RIGHTS WATCH

Human Rights Watch conducts regular, systematic investigations of human rights abuses in some seventy countries around the world. Our reputation for timely, reliable disclosures has made us an essential source of information for those concerned with human rights. We address the human rights practices of governments of all political stripes, of all geopolitical alignments, and of all ethnic and religious persuasions. Human Rights Watch defends freedom of thought and expression, due process and equal protection of the law, and a vigorous civil society; we document and denounce murders, disappearances, torture, arbitrary imprisonment, discrimination, and other abuses of internationally recognized human rights. Our goal is to hold governments accountable if they transgress the rights of their people.

Human Rights Watch began in 1978 with the founding of its Europe and Central Asia division (then known as Helsinki Watch). Today, it also includes divisions covering Africa, the Americas, Asia, and the Middle East. In addition, it includes three thematic divisions on arms, children's rights, and women's rights. It maintains offices in New York, Washington, Los Angeles, London, Brussels, Moscow, Dushanbe, Rio de Janeiro, and Hong Kong. Human Rights Watch is an independent, nongovernmental organization, supported by contributions from private individuals and foundations worldwide. It accepts no government funds, directly or indirectly.

The staff includes Kenneth Roth, executive director; Michele Alexander, development director; Reed Brody, advocacy director; Carroll Bogert, communications director; Cynthia Brown, program director; Barbara Guglielmo, finance and administration director; Jeri Laber special advisor; Lotte Leicht, Brussels office director; Patrick Minges, publications director; Susan Osnos, associate director; Jemera Rone, counsel; Wilder Tayler, general counsel; and Joanna Weschler, United Nations representative. Jonathan Fanton is the chair of the board. Robert L. Bernstein is the founding chair.

The regional directors of Human Rights Watch are Peter Takirambudde, Africa; José Miguel Vivanco, Americas; Sidney Jones, Asia; Holly Cartner, Europe and Central Asia; and Hanny Megally, Middle East and North Africa. The thematic division directors are Joost R. Hiltermann, arms; Lois Whitman, children's; and Regan Ralph, women's.

The members of the board of directors are Jonathan Fanton, chair; Lisa Anderson, Robert L. Bernstein, William Carmichael, Dorothy Cullman, Gina Despres, Irene Diamond, Adrian W. DeWind, Fiona Druckenmiller, Edith Everett, James C. Goodale, Jack Greenberg, Vartan Gregorian, Alice H. Henkin, Stephen L. Kass, Marina Pinto Kaufman, Bruce Klatsky, Alexander MacGregor, Josh Mailman, Samuel K. Murumba, Andrew Nathan, Jane Olson, Peter Osnos, Kathleen Peratis, Bruce Rabb, Sigrid Rausing, Anita Roddick, Orville Schell, Sid Sheinberg, Gary G. Sick, Malcolm Smith, Domna Stanton, Maureen White, and Maya Wiley. Robert L. Bernstein is the founding chair of Human Rights Watch.

CONTENTS

ACKNOWLEDGMENTS vii

I. SUMMARY AND RECOMMENDATIONS 1
    Torture, "Disappearances," and Extrajudicial Executions 3
    Human Rights Deficiencies in Mexico's Justice System 8
    Shades of Justice 10
    The Mexican Government's Approach to Human Rights 12
    Recommendations 16

II. PERSISTENT VIOLATIONS IN A CHANGING MEXICO 24
    The Government's Approach to Human Rights Violations 24
    The Government's Response to Human Rights Criticism 26
    The National Human Rights Commission 28
    The National Human Rights Program 29

III. HUMAN RIGHTS AND THE JUSTICE SYSTEM IN MEXICO 32
    Mexico's Justice System 32
    Investigating Crimes and Prosecuting Criminals 34
    The Public Defender's Office and "Person of Confidence" 35
    Human Rights Protections Under Mexican Law 36
        Constitutional and procedural guarantees 36
        The importance of individual and procedural guarantees 38
    Human Rights Deficiencies in Mexican Law and Legal Precedent 39
    Responsibility for Ensuring the Protection of Human Rights 45
    Judicial Reforms in Mexico 46

IV. MEXICO'S INTERNATIONAL HUMAN RIGHTS OBLIGATIONS .. 53
    Torture 53
    "Disappearance" 54
    Extrajudicial Execution 56
    Violations of Procedural Guarantees 57
    Responsibility to Ensure the Full Exercise of Human Rights and an Effective
        Remedy for Violations 57
    Rehabilitation for and Compensation to Victims of Violations 59
    International Standards on Police Actions and Use of Force 60
    Federal Responsibility for Violations by State or Local Authorities 61

V. TORTURE AND EXTRAJUDICIAL EXECUTION IN
   TAMAULIPAS STATE 63
   Juan Lorenzo Rodríguez Osuna 63
   José Alfredo Ponce Reyes 68
   Erick Cárdenas Esqueda 72
   The National Human Rights Commission in Tamaulipas 73
      Police and torture 73
      Medical exams 75
      Prosecutors and torture 76
      Additional cases documented by the CNDH 77

VI. TORTURE AND EXTRAJUDICIAL EXECUTION IN
    OAXACA STATE 79
    The Loxicha Region: Abuses in the Search for EPR Suspects 80
       Illegal detention, forced confession, and torture 80
       Extrajudicial execution 82
    The National Human Rights Commission in Oaxaca 85
    Additional Cases Documented by the CNDH 86

VII. "DISAPPEARANCES" AND THE JUSTICE SYSTEM 88
     Alejandro Hodoyán 90
     Fausto Soto Miller 94
     "Disappearance" and the Failure of the Morelos State Justice System .. 97
     The Suspected "Disappearance" of Verber, Verber, and Beltrán 100

VIII. IMPUNITY AND PUNISHMENT FOR HUMAN RIGHTS VIOLATIONS
      IN MEXICO 102
      Shades of Justice 104
      Overcoming Obstacles in Human Rights Cases 105
      Cases Deemed Successful by the PGR 106
      Cases Deemed Successful by the Foreign Ministry 110
      Success and Failure in Two Cases Handled by NGOs 112
      Human Rights Commission of the Federal District 114

IX. THE ROLE OF THE INTERNATIONAL COMMUNITY 116
    United States Human Rights Policy Toward Mexico 117
       Policies and assistance 117
       Human rights concerns with U.S. assistance to Mexico 119
    The European Union 120
    The United Nations and the Organization of American States 122

ACKNOWLEDGMENTS

Joel Solomon, research director for the Americas, researched and wrote this report, drawing on information gathered during fact-finding missions to Mexico City and the states of Baja California, Oaxaca, and Tamaulipas between September 1996 and June 1998. Deputy Director for the Americas Anne Manuel, Program Director Cynthia Brown, and Associate Counsel Joanne Mariner edited the manuscript. Human Rights Watch General Counsel Wilder Tayler and Americas division Director José Miguel Vivanco also reviewed the text. We are grateful to Human Rights Watch Americas division Advisory Board members Profs. Alejandro Garro and Paul Chevigny for providing valuable comments on this report. We also owe thanks to Prof. Herman Schwartz for his helpful comments on a very early draft. We are indebted to Víctor Brenes, Marisol López, Pilar Noriega, Digna Ochoa, and Salvador Tinajero, who kindly took the time to review the first three chapters of this report, and to Prof. Miguel Sarre, for his valuable observations on chapter three.

The author would particularly like to thank the many people, both victims and their family members, who shared their painful experiences during interviews. Their courage in the face of injustice animates this report.

Human Rights Watch gratefully recognizes the invaluable support of our Mexican colleagues. From the inception of this project in 1996, Mexican human rights groups have given important feedback on the scope and goals of the report. In addition, they aided tremendously in our field work, generously sharing their contacts, files, and expertise. We owe special thanks to the Reynosa, Tamaulipas-based Center for Border Studies and Promotion of Human Rights and the Tijuana, Baja California-based Binational Center for Human Rights. In Oaxaca, defense lawyer Israel Ochoa helped with cases. The following Mexico City-based groups, listed in alphabetical order, also provided crucial support: the "All Rights for All" Network of Civil Human Rights Organizations, Christian Action to Abolish Torture, the Fray Francisco de Vitoria Center for Human Rights, the Mexican Commission for the Defense and Promotion of Human Rights, and the Miguel Agustín Pro Juárez Center for Human Rights. In Washington, DC, the Center for Justice and International Law provided important feedback and case-related support.

We would also like to thank the many state and federal government officials who took the time to meet with and provide information to us.

I. SUMMARY AND RECOMMENDATIONS

Torture, "disappearances," and extrajudicial executions remain widespread in Mexico, despite numerous legal and institutional reforms adduced by successive Mexican governments as evidence of their commitment to protecting human rights. Indeed, reforms have taken place, but they have failed to abate, much less resolve, these serious, seemingly intractable problems. In part, this is because political leaders have been unwilling to ensure that existing human rights-related laws are applied vigorously; authorities are more likely to close ranks and deny that even well-documented abuses ever took place than they are to insist that those responsible be brought to justice.

The problem, however, runs far deeper than official toleration of abuses and impunity. Human rights violations also stem from the justice system's ineffective protection of individual guarantees and its lax approach to human rights abuses. Through willful ignorance of abuses or purposeful fabrication of evidence, prosecutors routinely prosecute victims using evidence obtained through human rights violations, including torture and illegal detention, and judges avail themselves of permissive law and legal precedent to condemn victims while ignoring abuses. Faced with this deeply troubling reality, the Mexican government has opted to treat human rights as an issue to be managed politically, countered with facile statistics, or handled through insufficient reforms or initiatives.

Based on research conducted over two years, this report documents cases of torture, "disappearance," and extrajudicial execution in five Mexican states, examining the violent abuses committed by police or soldiers and the actions of political leaders, prosecutors, and judges that followed. It demonstrates how and why the formal system of human rights protections in Mexico fails as victims pass from the hands of police or soldiers to prosecutors and judges. The cases permit an analysis of three interrelated stages in human rights cases: violations of individual guarantees prior to violent abuse, including illegal arrest and detention in excess of legally mandated limits; the violent human rights violations that followed, such as torture and "disappearance"; and the way prosecutors and judges dealt with the victims, including their use of confessions that followed improper or prolonged detention or torture and the citation by judges of legal precedent allowing them to avoid questioning such evidence. The Mexican government has failed to structure the justice system—understood to encompass police, prosecutors, and the courts—such that the goals of investigating crimes and punishing criminals are consonant with the aims of protecting human rights and promoting the rule of law. This failure is evident whether the victim is a suspected robber, accused drug trafficker, or alleged leftist guerrilla.

The victims of the abuses analyzed in this report suffer not only the physical and psychological trauma linked to their experiences, just as their family members, grieving for an executed or "disappeared" loved one, endure not only the pain of their loss or uncertainty about the victim's fate. In the face of such torment, victims and their family members must also abide a justice system more likely to prosecute the victim using evidence obtained through abuse than it is to see the perpetrators sent to prison. Indeed, it was the double affront of torture, "disappearance," and extrajudicial execution accompanied by the active or tacit complicity of prosecutors and judges that led Human Rights Watch to begin this project.

The problem is limited neither geographically nor by the type of crime imputed to the victim. To establish the territorial breadth of the justice system's failure, we drew case studies from the poor and predominantly rural south of Oaxaca, the industrialized central region of Morelos and Jalisco, and the northern border states of Baja California and Tamaulipas. To demonstrate the variety of circumstances in which the justice system fails, we scrutinized cases that took place in incidents related to counterinsurgency, drugs, and common crime.

Mexico's geographic diversity and complex political and judicial structures make it impossible to assert that a single government agency is responsible for committing or tolerating the vast array of human rights violations that take place—the evidence points at times to state or federal authorities, police or army officials, prosecutors, medical personnel, or judges. Some abuses are committed in a local context, while others are carried out in the name of the national interest. These complexities, however, should not detract from one fundamental reality: Mexico's federal government is obligated under international law to ensure that all people under its jurisdiction are able to fully exercise their human rights, to be free from torture and other abuses, and to have effective access to judicial remedies when violations take place. When such violations occur, the federal government is responsible. At the same time, the government must ensure that the agents responsible for committing violations are brought to justice. Based on the American Convention on Human Rights and the International Covenant on Civil and Political Rights, both of which Mexico has ratified, this norm applies whether the party responsible for the human rights violation is federal, state, or municipal.

To understand why the government has failed to address adequately Mexico's human rights violations, this report reviews official rhetoric on human rights and recent human rights-related legal and institutional reforms. It also addresses the National Program for the Promotion and Strengthening of Human Rights, which was announced by federal authorities in late December 1998. Largely since the election of President Carlos Salinas de Gortari (1988-1994), Mexico's highest-ranking political leaders have acknowledged that human rights violations take place, and important reforms have been undertaken. Among the positive changes must be counted the creation in 1990 of the National Human Rights Commission

(Comisión Nacional de Derechos Humanos, CNDH), which has often played a very important role in promoting respect for human rights in specific cases and on thematic issues; the passage of the 1991 Federal Law to Prevent and Punish Torture and subsequent constitutional reforms that bolstered the rights of detainees; and electoral reforms prior to the July 1997 elections, which were fundamental in permitting the freest elections ever held in Mexico.

Unfortunately, egregious human rights violations have persisted despite such measures. By documenting abuses, then following the victims through the justice system, this report sheds light on how and why the Mexican government's stated policy of protecting human rights and punishing human rights violators has failed. At the same time, the report includes recommendations for Mexican authorities, foreign governments, and international organizations.

Torture, "Disappearances," and Extrajudicial Executions

Human rights violations related to the real or assumed political affiliation of victims, or their purported allegiance to a leftist guerrilla group, tend to receive greater press attention in Mexico and abroad than those committed in other contexts, such as drug trafficking and common crime. Politically motivated cases of human rights violations, however, are by no means the only, or even the most common, cases in which abuses occur in Mexico. Three Tamaulipas state cases investigated in detail by Human Rights Watch, for instance, show the breakdown of the state justice system in cases of common crime, including robbery, murder, and possession of drugs. State authorities not only failed to provide proper oversight in these cases, they justified the actions of their subordinates.

All the force of the prosecutor's office was thrown against Juan Lorenzo Rodríguez Osuna, a victim of arbitrary detention and torture who was wrongly prosecuted and found guilty of murder. For two years at this writing, his family has fought for justice, as Rodríguez Osuna has languished in prison.

In Tamaulipas, the Rodríguez Osuna case most clearly demonstrates the inadequacy of the court's handling of human rights issues. The state judge who sentenced Rodríguez Osuna on murder charges went out of her way to exclude evidence that favored him, while admitting incriminating evidence obtained under conditions that violated human rights standards. For instance, she admitted a statement made by an alleged accomplice of Rodríguez Osuna even though the declarant retracted the statement on the grounds that he signed it under psychological torture and without his lawyers present. Several documents supposedly issued by the court were in fact written on the prosecutor's stationery, suggesting collusion between the prosecutor and judge.

A federal judge also sentenced Rodríguez Osuna on drug charges based solely on the same retracted statement made by the alleged accomplice, despite the fact that no physical evidence linked him to the drugs he was said to have possessed. A federal appeals court eventually overturned the drug conviction, but the prosecution and trial-level sentence demonstrated nonetheless the failure of the justice system to include adequate human rights criteria in prosecution and sentencing; the prosecution should never have gone forward in the first place.

This report's Tamaulipas state chapter also documents the case of José Alfredo Ponce Reyes, a victim of reckless police violence. Officers opened fire on Ponce Reyes then abandoned him when they believed him to be dead. Shot through the head, Ponce Reyes in fact survived but is confined to a wheelchair and unable to speak. For their part, the officers eventually walked free after providing contradictory statements to investigators. Before filing light charges against the police—"causing wounds" and "abuse of authority"—the prosecutor failed to interview a key witness who contradicted the police version of events.

In the case of Erick Cárdenas, Tamaulipas authorities failed to expend much energy at all investigating his torture and death in police custody. Arrested after an alleged street fight, Cárdenas was found dead in his cell soon after entering custody. Although officials insisted that he had hanged himself, the physical evidence, including signs of torture such as skinned testicles, suggested he was killed in jail. At the time that Human Rights Watch interviewed the victim's mother, a year after her son died, investigators had still not taken her testimony, even though she was one of the last people to see Cárdenas before the alleged street fight.

In contrast to Tamaulipas, many abuses in Oaxaca state stem from federal counterinsurgency efforts. Since 1996, the Popular Revolutionary Army (Ejército Popular Revolucionario, EPR) has operated there, carrying out bloody attacks on official targets. In response, civilian and military authorities have acted with a vengeance against suspected members of the armed group. A crackdown characterized by illegal detention, torture, and the extraction of confessions made under duress began in September of that year, focusing on the Loxicha region, where officials believed the EPR was particularly well organized. This report focuses on four torture and wrongful prosecution cases and an extrajudicial execution that took place during those operations. The picture that emerges is one of uncontrolled use of force in fighting the EPR compounded by a lack of concern on the part of officials throughout the justice system.

Victims in Oaxaca recounted to Human Rights Watch how police and soldiers carried out their work. After one day without food, for instance, one victim recalled, "They kept asking me to incriminate other people as members of the EPR

Summary and Recommendations

and to sign blank sheets of paper. I refused. It was there that they started to beat me. They stripped me and attached electrodes to my testicles." Finally, after more torture and threats against his family, the man signed blank pieces of papers. Rather than release him, however, as authorities promised, he was prosecuted and spent a year in jail before an appeals judge finally released him for lack of evidence. Other victims were prosecuted on evidence consisting of only hearsay and their own forced confessions. Some of the wrongly detained men were eventually released, in one case by a judge who refused to accept patently false statements—like those made in Spanish by a man who spoke only an indigenous language and had no translator.

It is encouraging that, on appeal, these men were released. Nonetheless, the prosecutor and trial-level judge accepted evidence that strongly suggested that it had been fabricated and the declarants tortured. Given that such problems are part of a pattern, not an anomaly, authorities cannot justify tolerating poor judicial processes on the grounds that the appeals process may correct them. The responsibility of the government to ensure that human rights standards are met during criminal investigations starts when the detainee enters custody and continues throughout the process.

To make matters worse in these Oaxaca cases, prosecutors ignored the torture suffered by detainees even when the victims managed to receive medical documentation showing that they had been tortured. Only after four such victims were eventually released did prosecutors begin to investigate their allegations of torture, but they did so because a Mexico City-based human rights group pushed them to and conducted much of the groundwork necessary for a prosecution to move forward. The prosecution has been seriously hampered by the delay of more than a year.

This report also documents the April 1997 extrajudicial execution in Oaxaca of Celerino Jiménez Almaraz. Police, who believed him to be linked to the EPR, claim he was killed in a shoot-out. The evidence, however, indicates he was chased from his home then shot at close range. Oaxaca state prosecutors initially assigned the case to police investigators from the same unit responsible for the killing. Seven months later, and only after sustained protest by a Mexico City human rights group, they switched jurisdiction for the investigation. Nonetheless, the investigation has moved slowly. At this writing, eighteen months have passed since the execution but, despite strong evidence, those responsible for the abuse remain free.

The "disappearance" cases documented in this report also demonstrate how serious abuses go unquestioned by prosecutors and judges. At the same time, they display the variety of contexts in which human rights violations take place in Mexico. "Disappearances"—secret, unacknowledged detentions followed by concealment of the victim's whereabouts, which might be temporary or prolonged—take place in circumstances related to Mexico's counterinsurgency campaign, counternarcotics initiatives, and common crime. "Disappearance" is a human rights violation that requires particularly urgent action by authorities, because it is so frequently accompanied by torture and murder. Quickly establishing the whereabouts of the victim in such cases can make the difference between freedom and prolonged suffering or death.

In the context of counternarcotics, three cases documented below demonstrate the failure of federal and state prosecutors to take seriously the crime of "disappearance," or worse, their ready prosecution of the victims without questioning how they came into official custody. In the case of Rogelio and Raúl Verber Campos and Cecilio Beltrán Cavada, from Baja California state, for instance, exactly one year passed between the time that family members filed a complaint about their "disappearance" with federal prosecutors in January 1997 and the time these relatives were interviewed about the case. State prosecutors who received a similar complaint never followed up at all. The whereabouts of the victims, believed to have been detained by the army, remain unknown.

In the cases of Alejandro Hodoyán and Fausto Soto Miller, the evidence shows that soldiers illegally detained the men separately and held them in unacknowledged detention beginning in September 1996. Both victims later reported weeks of torture. When soldiers were finished pumping Hodoyán and Soto Miller for information on a drug cartel, they turned them over to civilian prosecutors, who did not show the least concern for how they had come to be in military custody or the treatment they received there. Hodoyán was given immunity from prosecution and sent to the United States. U.S. officials, more interested in obtaining information on drug trafficking than in protecting human rights, became complicit in the initial "disappearance" of Hodoyán, even though the victim was a U.S. citizen. Weeks into his secret military detention, an agent of the U.S. Bureau of Alcohol, Tobacco, and Firearms (ATF) interviewed Hodoyán in custody, recognizing that the man was being held illegally. Hodoyán eventually identified himself as a U.S. citizen, and the ATF agent reported the situation to the U.S. Embassy, but nothing was ever done to aid the victim, despite his family's desperate pleas to U.S. and Mexican officials for help. In fact, the interview with the ATF agent led to greater U.S. interest in officially obtaining information from Hodoyán, and he was eventually transferred from military custody to Mexican prosecutors in Mexico City to U.S. prosecutors in San Diego, California. Hodoyán fled the United States and, once back in Mexico, was again "disappeared," this time after being picked up by a group of men that included a person identified by

Summary and Recommendations

Hodoyán's mother, who witnessed the abduction, as a federal police agent; Hodoyán's whereabouts remain unknown at the time of this writing.

Soto Miller was also turned over to prosecutors, but unlike Hodoyán, he was swiftly prosecuted. Based on what appears to be a fabricated story, officials charged him with drug-related crimes they said he committed while, all indications suggest, he was in fact in unacknowledged military detention. He was sentenced to forty years in prison. The Mexican federal attorney general's office did not respond to written questions submitted by Human Rights Watch on the Hodoyán and Soto Miller cases.

If the Verber Campos-Beltrán Cavada case shows the failure of state and federal prosecutors to investigate "disappearances" and the Hodoyán and Soto Miller cases demonstrate the active complicity of the federal attorney general's office, the Morelos state cases documented in this report describe a third type of responsibility on the part of the Mexican government: the failure to ensure that state-level justice systems function properly. In Morelos, state police ran a kidnapping ring and benefited from the tolerance of prosecutors, who failed to investigate the kidnappings or related "disappearances" by the police. In January 1998, federal authorities finally stepped in to prosecute Morelos state officials who ran or covered up the kidnapping ring, which turned out to be led by the state's anti-kidnapping police unit. That month, the leader of the anti-kidnapping police was caught trying to dispose of the body of a kidnapping victim who had died unexpectedly, which led to intense national and international press attention. Only after the scandal did authorities act, despite prior accounts of wrongdoing by Morelos state police and prosecutors.

The anatomy of the Morelos police operation is shown in the José Alberto Guadarrama García case, documented below. Morelos anti-kidnapping police "disappeared" Guadarrama García in March 1997, but prosecutors failed to move against one officer in the unit even after gathering substantial evidence to implicate him. Seven months after Guadarrama's abduction, and after intense pressure from Mexican and international human rights groups and the Inter-American Commission on Human Rights, authorities sought and obtained an arrest warrant for the officer. By that time, however, the officer had fled.

In Mexico, a writ of *amparo*—a constitutional challenge to the actions of officials—should be the mechanism by which courts require authorities to produce "disappeared" people. In practice, however, amparo is ineffective because judges refuse to provide the writs unless it is clear where the victim is being held, officials fail to seek victims vigorously in cases in which writs have been issued, or the government agents responsible for the "disappearance" simply deny holding the victims.

Human Rights Deficiencies in Mexico's Justice System

Both in practice and *de jure*, Mexico's justice system is fundamentally ambiguous about what to do with evidence obtained during or following human rights violations, including illegal arrests and searches, prolonged detention, and torture or other forms of coercion. The problem is not so much that prosecutors and judges interested in working in concert with human rights standards can find no statutory basis for doing so. In fact, the constitution and laws on the books could be read to require the dismissal of evidence obtained through human rights violations and the prosecution of public officials guilty of accepting or admitting such evidence. The problem lies in the fact that the law is often vague on these issues, and courts often rule in favor of accepting impugned evidence.

With respect to evidence obtained through human rights violations, Mexican law is clearest on confessions made under torture. Such statements are invalid in court, although the prohibition on their use is not effectively enforced. Further, standards have not been developed to ensure that other coercive situations, such as arbitrary arrest, invalidate the evidence obtained through the abuse. Arbitrary arrest and detention in excess of the maximum time allowed by law are crimes committed by public servants, but they do not necessarily affect the legal status of the detainee once charged. Similarly, as Mexican courts have ruled, illegal arrest and detention do not necessarily constitute grounds for rejecting statements made during or afterward. As a result, federal and state prosecutors either fail to question police about the circumstances surrounding arrest and detention, or, to facilitate prosecution, they participate in the fabrication of evidence. For their part, judges disregard indications of police or prosecutorial wrongdoing.

Human Rights Watch does not assert that all prosecutors and judges accept human rights violations committed in the process of law-enforcement work and prosecution. This report includes analysis of court decisions rejecting the use of evidence obtained through abuse. Human Rights Watch seeks to underscore, however, that Mexico's laws and the interpretation given them by judges leave plenty of room for judges to ignore human rights abuses if they so desire. As the cases in this report indicate, they choose to do so all too often. The problem is threefold. First, the burden to prove coercion rests with witnesses, victims, and defendants, who often must try to establish what happened to them against the wishes of prosecutors. Given the inherently coercive nature of any detention, courts should insist that procedural safeguards—including how and when police are to turn over detainees to prosecutors, the amount of time detainees can remain in custody before being turned over to a judge, and the scrupulous observation of requirements that declarants be accompanied by a legal counsel or a "person of confidence"—are followed to minimize the chance that coercion will lead to false conclusions reached through the judicial process. At the same time, judges should insist that if violations of this type are alleged, prosecutors carry out an investigation of the allegations. Violations of these safeguards should lead to the presumption that subsequent statements were coerced; this presumption could then be reversed if prosecutors proved that no coercion took place.

Second, even if coercion is likely or proven to have taken place, many judges go out of their way to accept impugned evidence. Key to their ability to do so is the "principle of procedural immediacy"—the concept in Mexico that the first statement made by a detainee has greater value than later statements. In other Latin American countries, the principle is understood to establish that whatever statements are given before or during trial should be made in the presence of the person who will make the decision as to whether the defendant is innocent or guilty. This is because the judge can evaluate the statements within the controlled context in which they are made. In Mexico, however, the idea behind the principle is that a detainee's first official statement, made before a prosecutor, has less chance of being coached than later statements made before prosecutors or judges, even though in Mexico the reality has been that a detainee's first statement has a greater chance of being coerced. When a detainee goes before a judge and retracts a statement made to a prosecutor, claiming coercion, judges can cite this principle to avoid determining whether or not the detainee was coerced and without questioning the police and prosecutors who may be acting in bad faith. Judges cited this principle in four cases reviewed in this report, to the extreme in one Tamaulipas case of convicting a man solely on the basis of a retracted statement.

Finally, Mexico's system of public defenders is so notoriously weak—to the point that the United Nations (U.N.) special rapporteur on torture reported in 1998 that "the public defender cannot be relied on to defend"—that the existence of formal procedural guarantees provides few real protections for victims. In an attempt to diminish coercion in the taking of statements by prosecutors, in 1990 Mexico instituted a system of the "person of confidence"—an individual named by the accused to be present when any statement is made. In a legal system in which individual guarantees are routinely ignored by judges, however, this system, like that of the public defenders, fails to provide real safeguards.

Mexico must shift the attitude of police, prosecutors, and judges from an ends-justify-the-means approach to a rule-of-law approach: human rights violations suffered by suspects or other detainees must be deemed unacceptable under any circumstances, and Mexico must develop and apply standards to exclude from the judicial process evidence obtained through abuse. The inadmissability of evidence obtained through human rights violations would exclude unreliable evidence from the judicial process and, at the same time, provide a disincentive to abusive authorities who would see cases thrown out of court because of serious human rights violations committed during investigation or prosecution. To help ensure that all statements or confessions used in the judicial process are made freely, Mexico should promote constitutional changes that would give validity only to statements made before a judge.

Any effective government effort to eliminate from the judicial process evidence, statements, and confessions obtained through the violation of human rights must also include the establishment of an effective system of accountability for public servants, including police, prosecutors, and judges—ensuring, of course, that the independence of the judiciary is not compromised. At each stage of the process, well-documented, suspected, or reported abuses must be thoroughly investigated, and confirmed complaints should lead to the dismissal of evidence obtained by abusive practices. Mexico's judges should be given explicit responsibility for ensuring that witnesses, suspects, the accused, and the sentenced suffer no human rights violations. Already existing federal and state judicial councils—responsible for administering courts—must include human rights protection in their evaluation of judges. Prosecutors who commit or consent to violations should be punished by their superiors, but judges must also reject prosecutorial malfeasance. In turn, prosecutors must hold police responsible for abuses committed in the course of law-enforcement work. Mexican law already penalizes "crimes against the administration of justice," which could be interpreted to include the acceptance by prosecutors or judges of evidence obtained through human rights violations. Such standards could form the backbone of aggressive campaigns by the federal attorney general and judicial councils against those who continue to prosecute or sentence without giving due consideration to human rights concerns.

In consonance with the purposes of Mexican and international law, the government must ensure that human rights standards are applied in such a way that two mutually reinforcing goals are met. First, Mexico's justice system must eliminate evidence that is unreliable because it was coerced or fabricated. At the same time, the exclusion of illegally obtained evidence must serve the purpose of deterring police and prosecutorial misconduct, another fundamental policy objective of laws aimed at preventing torture and other abuses.

Shades of Justice

As pervasive and deeply rooted as Mexico's human rights problems are, it would be wrong to assert that no human rights violation is ever investigated, or that no violator is ever prosecuted, jailed, or even sentenced. To understand how and why the system so routinely fails, therefore, this report also examines cases in

Summary and Recommendations

which some progress on human rights was made. Toward this end, on numerous occasions in 1998 Human Rights Watch requested information from Mexico's Foreign Ministry and Office of the Federal Attorney General (Procuraduría General de la República, PGR) regarding human rights cases they deemed successful. We sought cases in which torture had been documented and the responsible state agent sentenced and jailed for the crime. Neither government agency provided Human Rights Watch with the name, much less the details, of any public official sentenced for torture, although they did provide a total of eight cases that showed some advances in prosecuting torturers. In three of those cases, police officials were in jail awaiting trial. In one, a prison guard who had been charged with torture had fled, and in the rest authorities had yet to be charged or judges had yet to issue arrest warrants.

Human Rights Watch documented three additional cases, not submitted by the government, in which advances of some sort were made. In one of them, four Mexico City public security police officers are serving sentences for an extrajudicial execution. The sentences followed intense lobbying by the victim's family and a Mexican human rights group. In another case, a Mexico City judicial police officer was sentenced to two years in prison for failing to stop a subordinate from torturing a detainee, but he was released after paying a fine. The torturer himself was detained and charged with torture but released after an error by the Mexico City prosecutor; federal authorities who could have charged the torturer chose not to. In the third case, Mexico City prosecutors charged a torturer with "abuse of authority" but amended the charges to reflect torture after Mexico City's official human rights commission urged them to do so. The officer responsible fled.

Human Rights Watch recognizes the breadth of penalties that can be applied to public servants who violate human rights—from administrative actions such as poor performance reviews, suspension from work, or firing to criminal prosecution. Given the severity of the cases documented in this report, however, authorities must vigorously pursue criminal prosecution of those responsible, in addition to any administrative sanctions they may apply. The penalties applied must be commensurate with the human rights crimes committed.

The obstacles to justice in human rights cases are immense in Mexico. In the eleven cases reviewed in which some progress was made, intense press attention, the insistence of victims' family members, or pressure from governmental or nongovernmental human rights groups played a key role. In ten of the cases, human rights groups essentially carried out the investigative work that prosecutors failed to do, documenting both the foot-dragging or covering-up that took place and the evidence of abuse that authorities sought to ignore. Even that was often not enough, however. Prosecutors had to be pushed to move cases forward.

The sheer number of abuses in Mexico makes it impossible for human rights organizations to take action on all cases. It is the rare case that receives the time, money, and energy needed to ensure that prosecutors take the incremental steps necessary to see justice done. Foot-dragging is an effective strategy on the part of authorities uninterested in prosecuting human rights violators, both because new cases will undoubtedly come along to distract even the most committed nongovernmental human rights groups and because time diminishes the likelihood that valuable evidence, including the physical markings of torture and the testimony of victims and witnesses, will be available. The CNDH plays an important role in ensuring that otherwise forgotten cases receive attention. However, it handles only a portion of Mexico's human rights cases and does not track the final outcome of the cases on which it works, so no reliable information exists linking its labor to the final disposition of human rights violators.

To overcome these serious obstacles, political leaders must shed their reticence to take action against state agents who commit human rights violations. They must do much more than make pronouncements of concern about human rights in general. The prosecution of human rights violators must be actively and publicly promoted. At the same time, the CNDH and PGR should develop systems to track human rights cases from inception to completion, including the sentences issued by judges, so that reliable statistics and case information are available nationally showing how such cases are handled and why impunity is such a problem in Mexico.

The Mexican Government's Approach to Human Rights

President Ernesto Zedillo has recognized that human rights violations take place in Mexico, but his government, like those of his predecessors, has not been willing to recognize the breadth of the problem or to systematically promote the prosecution of the state agents responsible for abuses. Mexican and international human rights organizations, intergovernmental human rights agencies, and the government's own National Human Rights Commission have documented serious and widespread human rights violations that still receive scant attention from Mexican policy-makers. Individual cases of abuse are more likely to be ignored or denied than resolved, and the government selectively rejects what it deems foreign intervention in its human rights affairs. Nonetheless, the Zedillo administration has also made noteworthy advances, such as finally recognizing the jurisdiction of the Inter-American Court of Human Rights in late 1998.

On December 21, 1998, the federal government announced the National Program for the Promotion and Strengthening of Human Rights. The program was touted as an initiative conceived to achieve eight overall goals, including the consolidation of a culture of respect for human rights and of the institutional entities responsible for protecting them, the design of mechanisms to identify positive and negative aspects of Mexican human rights policy, and the dissemination of information about human rights. Several of the specific proposals contained in the program would indeed constitute important contributions to the protection and promotion of human rights, provided that authorities take the issues more seriously in the future than they have in the past.

While laudable in its recognition of the need for such a program and its inclusion of an array of government agencies, it suffers inherent weaknesses. For example, it does not describe the government's diagnosis of the human rights violations that take place in Mexico. It provides no reflection on how serious and widespread they are, why they take place, or why prior attempts to resolve them have failed. Without establishing priorities, it refers in only general terms to human rights abuses such as torture and impunity, and calls on public servants to counter them. If the program is to succeed, it must have a clearly defined sense of the problem before attempting to resolve it; given that federal authorities have tended to minimize the seriousness of human rights violations in Mexico, it is not clear that such a sense exists or, if it does, that it accurately reflects the true nature of human rights violations in the country. In this regard, detailed prior consultations with Mexican governmental and nongovernmental human rights organizations would have been valuable but did not take place.

To its credit, the current Mexican administration has allowed unprecedented access to Mexico by U.N. and Organization of American States (OAS) human rights bodies, including the U.N. special rapporteur on torture, who visited Mexico in 1997, and the OAS's Inter-American Commission on Human Rights, which carried out an on-site study in 1996; both issued comprehensive reports in 1998 based on their findings. The government also invited the U.N. high commissioner for human rights to visit the country.

Nonetheless, this openness has not been accompanied by a willingness to recognize publicly the scope of the problems identified by these international bodies or to follow their recommendations. The government, for instance, has steadfastly refused to comply with recommendations made by the OAS commission in specific cases in which it found that Mexico had committed human rights violations. At this writing, the government had taken no appreciable steps to implement recommendations contained in the comprehensive reports published by the U.N. special rapporteur or the Inter-American Commission on Human Rights.

The government is often quick to counter human rights criticism with facile statistics. When the U.N. Committee against Torture discussed Mexico in 1997, for example, the Foreign Ministry responded by asserting that there is no impunity for torturers in Mexico because 69 percent of the CNDH's recommendations on 105 torture cases had been fully implemented and another 30 percent had been partially fulfilled. Citation of CNDH statistics, however, was meaningless regarding what actually happened to people accused of torture, since CNDH recommendations typically call for prosecutors to open an investigation, a recommendation that can be completely fulfilled without significantly moving an investigation forward. In fact, the CNDH does not track what happens to perpetrators once they are charged. Human Rights Watch's review of CNDH torture cases from Oaxaca and Tamaulipas—included in the respective chapters covering abuses in these states—shows, in fact, that most officials accused of torture by the CNDH never go to jail.

Criticism of the misleading use of CNDH statistics should not be confused with criticism of the CNDH itself. The government's federal commission has often played an important role in documenting abuses in specific cases and on thematic issues. Many cases that never receive public attention are moved forward after commission intervention. At this writing, legislative initiatives are pending in Mexico to increase the independence of the CNDH vis-à-vis the executive, which has always exercised control over its budget and named its president. The CNDH is not as consistent in tackling cases as it could be, and its mandate does not include labor-related or electoral human rights issues. Perhaps its greatest weakness, however, stems from the fact that its recommendations have no binding force on the authorities who receive them and it has not developed an effective way to shame officials into complying. Similarly, Mexico's Congress has not used CNDH recommendations to pressure federal authorities or state governors to improve their human rights records.

If the Mexican government has been ineffective in countering human rights violations, it is not for lack of human rights guarantees in the constitution or legislation expressly protecting against certain abuses, like torture. Indeed, in some areas, guarantees have been strengthened in recent years. Most important were constitutional amendments in 1993 that removed legal value from testimonies taken by judicial police. In an effort to eliminate police abuse of detainees, the reforms established that only statements made before a prosecutor or judge could be used in court. At the same time, the constitutional reforms established that it would be a crime for prosecutors not to ensure that detainees had legal representation during pre-trial proceedings; prior to the change, detainees had a right to request a lawyer in such circumstances, but if they did not expressly ask for one, prosecutors did not have to make sure one was present. The 1991 Federal Law to Prevent and Punish Torture, which is binding for federal public servants, expressly establishes that no

Summary and Recommendations 15

confessions made under torture are accepted in court. These initiatives were positive but insufficient to resolve Mexico's serious human rights problems.

Some constitutional changes, however, have weakened human rights safeguards, and new reforms pending at this writing stand to further deteriorate human rights conditions in Mexico. In 1994 and 1995, for instance, reforms gave prosecutors greater latitude to carry out arrests without court order. In December 1997, President Zedillo sent a package of reforms to Congress designed to fight crime, a growing concern in Mexico. Arguing that criminals are more sophisticated now than in the past, the president's proposals included measures such as making it easier for prosecutors to press charges against suspects with less evidence—to the point of not requiring proof that a crime had even been committed—and allowing police to consider a suspect "caught in the act" if the suspect was found up to seventy-two hours after the crime was committed. Given that Mexico's procedural safeguards are already ineffective, the changes would merely increase the chances that people were wrongly prosecuted.

In September 1998, President Zedillo announced a National Crusade Against Crime based on the proposed legal reforms; to complement the reforms, the government announced what it called "Strategies and Actions of the National Public Security Program," consisting of eight subjects on which federal and state authorities would focus attention in order to fight crime. Training, hiring more law enforcement and court personnel, and establishing centralized data bases were among the steps promised by the government. Funding would be increased to reach these goals. Several of the proposals to fight crime, such as creation of new nationwide data bases and expanding citizen participation in oversight of police, would lend themselves to the protection of human rights.

The public security and human rights programs announced by the federal government may work at cross-purposes, however, when it comes to promoting human rights. The former is premised on a belief that the current state of crime in Mexico demands limiting individual guarantees, a formula likely to lead to greater abuses. Although the human rights program notes that better training of police under the security initiative will lead to greater respect for human rights, this report demonstrates that the government must integrate detailed human rights strategies into its law-enforcement initiatives.

Months after it announced its strategies for fighting crime, the federal government said in November that it would create a new police force, called Federal Preventive Police, designed to prevent crimes of a federal nature and to assist federal judicial police in carrying out investigations. Before moving forward with the creation of a new police force, the government should publicly provide a clear strategy for ensuring that human rights violations committed by these officers will be investigated and that the offending authorities will be prosecuted. The new police force offers an opportunity to include mechanisms from the outset that will ensure the protection and promotion of human rights.

Mexico's pattern of negligence in ensuring that human rights protections are effective amounts to a policy of permission for those safeguards to fail. Missing from the government's human rights strategy is attention to specific cases of human rights violations and the structural deficiencies that facilitate them. Rather than denounce human rights violators and insist that they be brought to justice, the government points to the formal laws and structures that should protect human rights as a measure of its commitment. Instead of insisting that procedural guarantees be scrupulously followed, the Zedillo administration is pushing to loosen those guarantees. The starting point for the government's strategy for promoting human rights must be recognition that Mexico's formal human rights protections are not effective because laws, practice, and legal precedent conspire against them.

Recommendations

To the Federal Government of Mexico:
Toward the development of a national human rights strategy

1) The federal government should reformulate its National Program for the Promotion and Strengthening of Human Rights to clearly and publicly specify the exact nature and cause of the human rights violations that are the program's subject, describe how serious and widespread they are, and explain why prior attempts to resolve them have failed. In a prior diagnostic phase, as in subsequent initiatives designed to address human rights violations, the government should seek input from governmental and nongovernmental human rights organizations. The program should contain a timetable for achieving its goals and should seek to develop consensus within Mexico regarding the nature of human rights violations and the best way to address them.

2) President Zedillo should match his rhetorical commitment to human rights protection and promotion of the rule of law with an action-oriented policy of tolerating no human rights violations. Prosecutors must be instructed to swiftly investigate and prosecute suspected human rights violators, and their bosses must be held accountable if they do not. Federal funding destined for

Summary and Recommendations

state governments should be used as a lever to press state governors to adopt positive human rights measures of their own.

Toward the development of a human rights legislative agenda

3) The government should promote legislation to "federalize" the crimes of torture, extrajudicial execution, and "disappearance" such that these crimes would be under federal jurisdiction regardless of the official responsible. The government should also federalize cases of grossly abusive arbitrary detention that lead to violations of the right to life or physical integrity.

4) The government should promote legislation that would give federal authorities responsibility for prosecuting human rights cases of any type if it determines that a systematic or widespread practice of such violations takes place within a state and that state officials routinely fail to prosecute them. As part of such a program, the federal government should take all necessary steps to ensure that the state justice system is strengthened to the point of being able to adequately handle human rights cases, at which time authority for prosecuting human rights cases would be returned to state officials. The government should develop clear and public guidelines for determining when a systematic or widespread practice takes place and when a state justice system would be deemed capable of reassuming jurisdiction over cases of human rights violations.

5) The government, after consulting with governmental and nongovernmental human rights organizations, should develop legislation that would exclude from judicial processes evidence obtained through human rights violations, including torture and "disappearance" and serious cases of arbitrary or prolonged detention. Given the difficulty victims sometimes have in proving torture or coercion, the legislation should include an express statutory presumption of coercion for statements or confessions obtained following prolonged detention.

6) To minimize the opportunity and rationale for police and prosecutors to coerce detainees, federal authorities should promote reforms requiring the presence of a judge for any declarations to have legal value as evidence.

7) The federal government should evaluate its National Crusade Against Crime with an eye toward ensuring that measures proposed and adopted do not limit the rights of suspects.

8) Legislation should be promoted to criminalize "disappearances" and to ensure that the statute of limitations for the crimes of torture, "disappearance," and extrajudicial execution are substantial and in accordance with the gravity of these crimes.

Toward the development of more effective institutions

9) The PGR should establish a system to closely track the progress and outcome of human rights prosecutions and the performance of prosecutors in such cases. Judges' sentences in such cases should be reviewed to discern the ways in which prosecutions succeed or fail, so that more effective prosecutorial strategies can be developed. The work of prosecutors in human rights cases should be part of their official job evaluations.

10) As the government considers the development of data bases related to human rights issues, it should ensure that they are designed to track complaints and the outcome of complaints. Data bases should be designed in consultation with governmental and nongovernmental human rights organizations. The tracking of CNDH recommendations should be in addition to the tracking of complaints within the PGR and other government agencies.

11) The federal government should promote reforms to the Federal Judicial Council that would give the council explicit responsibility for reviewing the work of judges as it relates to human rights. The council should document cases in which judges accept evidence obtained through human rights violations or otherwise fail to ensure that procedural or individual guarantees are observed throughout the legal processes in cases that come before them. Appropriate administrative or criminal punishment should be pursued against judges who do not adequately handle human rights violations in the cases that come before them. Funding should be provided to enable monitoring and follow-up.

12) The government should develop mechanisms to permit strong, independent monitoring of police and detention facilities. It should strengthen the independence of authorities in a position to evaluate the human rights-

Summary and Recommendations 19

related actions of law-enforcement personnel, such as medical examiners in police and prison facilities, so that they work independently from prosecutors and police. The government should facilitate the establishment of community-based boards to oversee the work of police and channel complaints to authorities; they should be permitted to monitor police detention centers. Unannounced inspections of detention centers should be permitted.

13) The government should overhaul the public defenders' institution to ensure that public defenders are equipped, trained, sufficiently independent, and paid enough to ensure an adequate defense of their clients.

14) The CNDH should closely track the final outcome of the cases it documents, including which government officials ultimately serve prison sentences based on CNDH documentation. The CNDH should also develop strategies for increasing public pressure on government officials who fail to carry out CNDH recommendations.

15) Before moving forward with the creation of a new Federal Preventive Police, the government should publicly announce a clear strategy for ensuring that human rights violations committed by these officers will be investigated and that the offending authorities will be prosecuted. Such a strategy could include mechanisms to incorporate human rights criteria in the job-performance reviews of officers and to develop a data base of human rights complaints and investigations relating to them.

Regarding the international community

16) The Mexican government should comply with the rulings of the Inter-American Commission on Human Rights regarding specific cases, such as that of Gen. Francisco Gallardo, the Ejido Morelia case, and Aguas Blancas. It should announce publicly a detailed plan for complying with recommendations made in the commission's September 1998 report on the human rights situation in Mexico.

17) The Mexican government should follow up the general request that it made for technical assistance from the United Nations Commission on Human Rights with actions designed to develop a specific and far-reaching program to be implemented as soon as possible. The program should include an evaluation of the ways in which Mexico's legal system fails to adequately

address human rights violations, despite formal human rights protections included in the law.

18) The Mexican government should follow up its stated intention to invite the United Nations special rapporteur on extrajudicial, summary, or arbitrary executions with a formal request for a visit as soon as possible.

19) The government should revise visa requirements for human rights monitors who wish to travel to Mexico to ensure that visas are given quickly and without conditions that would hamper their work, such as excessive limitation on the amount of time they can spend in the country. Similarly, monitors should not be required to provide detail about whom they plan to interview and the locations they plan to visit. The requirements should be clear and the subject of legislation, not simply established by internal regulations developed by the Ministry of Government.

To Mexico's Congress:

1) Mexico's Congress should ensure that the CNDH is able to function as an agency independent of the federal government.

2) Given that the federal government provides funding to states for multiple purposes, Congress should play a more active role in monitoring the human rights records of state governments with an eye toward developing transparent mechanisms that could condition federal aid to state governments that engage in a consistent pattern of gross human rights violations.

3) Mexico's Congress should urgently conduct a thorough review of Mexican legal precedents related to human rights, including the "principle of procedural immediacy," to identify those that effectively weaken human rights protections by allowing judges to avoid questioning evidence suspected to have been obtained through human rights violations. Legislation should be promoted that would address such doctrines.

4) Congress should enact legislation requiring the presence of a judge for a declaration to have any legal value as evidence.

5) Congress should enact legislation to criminalize "disappearances" and ensure that the statute of limitations for the crimes of torture,

"disappearance," and extrajudicial execution are substantial and in accordance with the gravity of these crimes.

6) Congress should pass legislation giving federal and state judicial councils responsibility for guaranteeing that judges properly ensure that procedural and human rights standards are observed throughout the legal processes in cases that come before them. Funding should be provided to ensure that monitoring and follow-up are possible.

To the United States Government:

1) The State Department should more publicly voice concern about human rights violations in Mexico and give the subject greater priority at bilateral meetings with Mexican government officials.

2) U.S. officials should be required to ensure that information they gather from sources in Mexico is obtained in strict accord with human rights standards and that any reasonable concern about human rights violations committed against sources is investigated.

3) The United States government should undertake an exhaustive investigation into the serious mishandling of the "disappearance" of U.S. citizen Alejandro Hodoyán to determine why U.S. embassy officials and law-enforcement agents took no action to assist him, though they knew that Hodoyán was in secret military custody. Further, the investigation should focus on how and why U.S. government officials later accepted custody of Hodoyán to debrief him about drug trafficking, even though his initial detention so blatantly violated the law. The results of the investigation should be made public, and effective measures should be implemented to prohibit similar cases in the future.

4) United States Agency for International Development (USAID) judicial exchange initiative in Mexico should include detailed analysis of the ways in which laws and legal practice in Mexico perpetuate human rights violations. Training designed to overcome such problems should be included in the program.

To the European Union:

1) Following the recommendation of several committees of the European Parliament, the Council of Ministers should instruct the European Commission to work with the Mexican government to ensure that funds for democracy and human rights projects, under Article 39 of the Agreement on Economic Partnership, Political Coordination, and Cooperation, become available as soon as possible.

2) The Council of Ministers should ensure that when the European Commission and representatives of member states work with the Mexican government on the annual evaluation of the implementation of the agreement, there will be an explicit review of the human rights situation in Mexico and Europe, as recommended by the European Parliament's committees on foreign affairs and cooperation and development.

3) The Council of Ministers should solicit written reports, to be made public, on the human rights situation in Mexico well in advance of the annual review of the agreement, thereby allowing both the council and European Parliament to evaluate the information received within the context of the review. The council should request documentation from all governmental and nongovernmental sources interested in supplying it. The Council of Ministers should hold public hearings at which these sources could explain their material and answer questions, as the European Parliament has already done.

4) The European Parliament should maintain the valuable attention it has paid to human rights in Mexico and, in particular, the ways in which the European Union can promote human rights there. It should continue to hold periodic hearings on human rights in Mexico and maintain Mexican human rights on its agenda for working with other bodies of the European Union.

5) The European Commission should name at least one full-time official in its mission in Mexico City to be responsible for documenting and reporting on the human rights situation in the country.

6) European Union member states represented in Mexico should undertake a coordinated effort to monitor and promote human rights in the country.

Summary and Recommendations 23

To the United Nations and the Organization of American States:

1) U.N. Secretary-General Kofi Annan and High Commissioner for Human Rights Mary Robinson should maintain the important attention they have given to Mexico during 1998. They should continue to reach out to Mexican human rights groups for information on human rights violations in the country.

2) High Commissioner Robinson should take the opportunity offered by the Mexican government's invitation to visit to develop a comprehensive diagnosis of Mexico's human rights problems. She should insist upon being permitted to develop and recommend effective measures to address those problems.

3) The Inter-American Commission on Human Rights should maintain its investigations into individual cases and should use its broad experience on Mexico to promote human rights reforms there. The commission should actively urge the Mexican government to act on the recommendations contained in its September 1998 comprehensive report on human rights in Mexico.

II. PERSISTENT VIOLATIONS IN A CHANGING MEXICO

The Government's Approach to Human Rights Violations

During the last twenty years, successive Mexican presidents have revamped and reorganized everything from the electoral system to the economy to the tax code, amending or jettisoning outdated laws and facilitating the country's increasing insertion into the global economy. Human rights and the administration of justice have also been the explicit subject of many reforms. Yet human rights violations remain widespread and serious in Mexico. In part, this seeming paradox can be explained by the government's consistent failure to ensure that laws designed to protect human rights are enforced and that human rights violators are prosecuted. The problem also stems from a justice system that, in practice, does not adequately reject and penalize the use of evidence obtained through human rights violations. And in part, Mexico's continuing human rights problems can be attributed to the government's preference for rhetoric designed to mollify domestic and international critics over action that would resolve specific human rights problems.

To bolster their case that Mexico assiduously protects human rights, authorities adduce a series of legal reforms and newly established institutions designed to protect human rights. The logical conclusion, as the Foreign Ministry argued in May 1997, is that, "Mexico has advanced in its fight against torture. Errors of the past have been corrected, and the path has been adjusted when it became evident that the strategies that were followed did not lead to the sought-after result."[1] In 1998 a new foreign minister joined the Mexican cabinet and immediately distinguished herself from her predecessor by demonstrating greater openness to dialogue with certain human rights entities. Nonetheless, the Foreign Ministry continued to insist that great strides had been made in protecting human rights. "During recent years, Mexico has made a great effort to strengthen the protection and enforceability of human rights," the ministry affirmed after the Inter-American Commission on Human Rights issued a report in September 1998 on human rights problems in Mexico. "This has been done through multiple reforms of domestic legislation and the creation or restructuring of the national institutions responsible for [human rights]. At the same time, intense efforts to combat and eradicate impunity have been undertaken."[2]

One way that authorities make this argument is by citing misleading statistics suggesting that serious abuses, like torture, are properly investigated and that their

---

[1] Foreign Ministry, press release 142, May 9, 1997. Translation by Human Rights Watch.

[2] Foreign Ministry, press release, September 28, 1998. Translation by Human Rights Watch.

authors are successfully prosecuted.[3] In May 1997 the Foreign Ministry cited CNDH figures to conclude, "It is very clear that there is no impunity in Mexico for acts of torture, because of the 105 National Human Rights Commission recommendations that proved that torture had taken place, seventy-two have been totally fulfilled and thirty-two are partially completed."[4]

The truth is that CNDH recommendations—findings in a specific case and the measures it deems necessary to resolve the problems encountered—are often counted as fulfilled without anyone actually being held accountable for abuses, since the recommendations frequently only call on prosecutors to open an investigation, not bring violators to justice. In fact, the CNDH cases from Tamaulipas and Oaxaca analyzed in this report demonstrate this very point. At the same time, CNDH statistics on torture are partial at best, since the entity does not tabulate torture cases documented by state human rights commissions and nongovernmental organizations (NGOs).

Indeed, the government's November 1996 report to the U.N. Committee against Torture briefly notes that of 1,022 recommendations issued by the CNDH from its inception in 1990 to the end of 1996, 105 proved that torture had taken place.[5] Only eight people were ever convicted of torture, however, and three of them were later acquitted.[6] In 1997, the Office of the Federal Attorney General informed the U.N. special rapporteur on torture that results from the 1990s were actually slightly worse, consisting of only four confirmed convictions.[7] In June

---

[3] Human Rights Watch recognizes that punishment for human rights violations can include sanctions in addition to prosecution, such as the levying of fines, suspension, or termination of employment. Given the seriousness of the crime of torture, however, the violation should be punished by prosecution in addition to any other administrative penalties applied.

[4] Foreign Ministry, press release 142, May 9, 1997. Translation by Human Rights Watch.

[5] United Nations, "Consideration of Reports Submitted by States Parties Under Article 19 of the Convention" (New York: United Nations Publications, November 27, 1996), CAT/C/34/Add.2, p. 16. The number of officials guilty of torture was likely to be much higher because in Mexico, torture is often carried out by more than one official at a time.

[6] Ibid.

[7] United Nations, "Question of the Human Rights of All People Submitted to Any Form of Detention or Imprisonment, in Particular: Torture and Other Cruel, Inhuman or Degrading Treatment or Punishment," (New York: United Nations Publications, January 14, 1998), E/CN.4/1998/38/Add.2, para. 56.

1998, the attorney general's office told Human Rights Watch that six people were serving sentences for torture.[8]

At the same time, authorities argue that great strides have been made in protecting human rights by citing the reform or creation of human rights-related laws and institutions, as did the Foreign Ministry in response to the 1998 report issued by the Inter-American Commission on Human Rights. This misleading argument on the part of government officials falsely equates the existence of laws and institutions with the effective application of those laws and the adequate functioning of those institutions. Although their existence is clearly positive, it is not enough to bring Mexico into line with its international human rights obligations. As described in this report's chapter on these obligations, Mexico must ensure that its human rights-related laws and institutions are *effective*.

The Government's Response to Human Rights Criticism

Mexican human rights groups, international organizations, other governments, and intergovernmental organizations have all strongly criticized Mexico's human rights practices. Depending on the source, timing, and topic of the criticism, the official response has varied—from hostile rejection to measured promise to study the problems identified.

When Rosario Green took the helm at the Foreign Ministry in January 1998, the ministry moved away from the knee-jerk rejection of all foreign comment on Mexican human rights problems that had characterized the tenure of her predecessor. While the swift and unequivocal dismissal of foreign comment still took place in some cases, as when U.N. High Commissioner for Human Rights Mary Robinson expressed concern about Chiapas in June 1998, a more measured response was given in other instances, including in reaction to the Inter-American Commission's 1998 Mexico study, which was greeted with a commitment to carefully analyze the report and its recommendations. The rejection of Robinson came amid intense political debate in Mexico over the government's handling of incidents in Chiapas and so may have been determined by its potential impact on the domestic political equation.[9]

The issue of human rights in Chiapas remained one of the most sensitive to government officials. Perhaps in response to the growing influence of human rights

---

[8] Human Rights Watch interview, Eduardo López Figueroa, director, Internal Affairs Bureau of the Office of the Federal Attorney General, Mexico City, June 12, 1998.

[9] The Foreign Ministry later invited Mary Robinson to visit Mexico. At this writing, neither the timing nor the agenda for the trip has been announced.

groups, Mexican officials strongly criticized local human rights organizations and tried to divide Mexican groups from their international counterparts. In July, for instance, President Zedillo lashed out at Mexican human rights groups in Chiapas, criticizing those who urged international human rights defenders to visit the state. He suggested that encouraging such visits was at odds with promoting respect for the constitution and the rule of law.[10]

The government also announced new restrictions on foreign human rights monitors conducting research in Mexico. In May 1998 the Ministry of Government developed new requirements for human rights visas, including a thirty-day waiting period, a ten-day maximum stay, and a maximum of ten people for any human rights delegation; the new rules provide for facilitated extension of visas in emergencies and for extending the trip beyond ten days in exceptional circumstances.

People soliciting visas must provide a "work plan," which, in practice, has led government officials to request details of all people to be interviewed and all communities to be visited. To receive a visa, the applicant must also submit a copy of the organization's articles of incorporation and must demonstrate that the group has either consultative status with the United Nations or has been in existence for at least five years. The decision on who will and will not receive a visa is now made by a centralized office in the Ministry of Government, not in each consulate, as before. The visa requirements are currently issued by the ministry, and they are not established by any law.

Although the Ministry of Government announced that the new rules would eliminate the arbitrary decision-making on visas that had been criticized by human rights groups, including Human Rights Watch, the new process is no less arbitrary. Members of human rights organizations who have applied for visas since the new requirements came into effect have reported confusing and contradictory responses from Mexican consular officials. Several delegations have reported having visa requests denied. During 1998, the Mexican government expelled numerous foreign observers for Chiapas without providing them even minimal due process.

To its credit, during 1998 Mexico recognized the jurisdiction of the Inter-American Court of Human Rights. It also announced in August 1998 that it would invite the U.N. special rapporteur on extrajudicial, summary, or arbitrary executions to visit Mexico. During 1996 and 1997, the government permitted

---

[10] Presidency of Mexico, "Versión Estenográfica de las palabras del presidente Ernesto Zedillo, durante la evaluación del Programa Estatal de Alfabetización, que encabezó en la Escuela Secundaria Técnica No. 42, de este municipio," Simojovel, Chiapas, July 1, 1998.

human rights investigative teams from the Inter-American Commission on Human Rights and the United Nations Committee against Torture to visit Mexico.

Even though the government has touted such visits as proof of its openness to human rights scrutiny, it has not acted on their recommendations. In fact, the Mexican government has expressly rejected findings of the Inter-American Commission on several Mexican cases, most notably that of Brig. Gen. Francisco Gallardo, who has languished in military prison since 1993 in retaliation for his call for greater respect for human rights within the Mexican army. Mexican military authorities charged the general with corruption and destruction of army property, court-martialed him, and sentenced him on March 11, 1998, to fourteen years and eight months in prison after the Inter-American Commission recommended his immediate release in 1996.[11] Similarly, the government failed to implement the commission's recommendations on the Ejido Morelia case, in which three men were detained and executed by soldiers in Chiapas state in 1994, the Manríquez case, analyzed in this report, and the Aguas Blancas case, in which police massacred seventeen people in Guerrero state in 1995.

The National Human Rights Commission

The CNDH has often been the subject of criticism, but it has unquestionably played an important role in promoting human rights in Mexico. The institution is most often criticized for its organic links to the executive branch of government; because its mandate restricts it from working on labor- or election-related human rights issues; and because its findings, published in the form of recommendations containing case details, are not obligatory. Indeed, the president of the CNDH is named by Mexico's president, and the institution's budget is entirely provided by the executive branch.[12] At this writing, it appears likely that the CNDH will be granted greater autonomy from the executive branch with respect to both its funding and the appointment of its president.

The CNDH's recommendations are not binding on those who receive them, and it has not developed any effective way to shame authorities into seeing that justice is done in cases it documents. There is no penalty, except political, if a government official fails to follow recommendations made by the commission. Relatively few CNDH cases, however, receive the political attention that would

---

[11] Inter-American Commission on Human Rights, "Report No. 43/96, Case 11.430," in Organization of American States, *Annual Report of the Inter-American Commission on Human Rights 1996* (Washington, DC: Organization of American States, 1997), p. 513.

[12] Human Rights Watch interview, Mireille Roccatti, president of the CNDH, Mexico City, June 5, 1998.

lead to the stigmatization of these officials. The CNDH does not publicize details on who, if anyone, went to jail because of a human rights violation documented by the institution. In fact, the commission does not even track such information, so there is no true measure of how the CNDH ultimately influences the justice system when it comes to human rights violations. Statistics produced by the CNDH—on the number of judicial investigations begun, the number of officials indicted, and the number of recommendations fulfilled by authorities—provide a glimpse of part of the judicial process but do not help analyze impunity in Mexico.

The commission was founded at a time when Mexico's human rights record was coming under greater international scrutiny than ever before, as the country prepared to begin negotiations for the North American Free Trade Agreement (NAFTA) and privatization of state-owned enterprises attracted international investment on an unprecedented scale. Indeed, the CNDH may very well have been conceived to feign an interest in human rights protection on the part of the government. However, the work of the commission on specific cases and issues shows that it has become much more than an adornment. Although it is not as consistent as it could be, in 1998 alone, the CNDH has released hard-hitting reports on torture and "disappearances" committed by the army and strongly criticized government actions against alleged supporters of the leftist Zapatista Army of National Liberation (Ejército Zapatista de Liberación Nacional, EZLN). In less visible cases, too, CNDH recommendations, although not binding, have led to positive developments.

The commission has the authority to compel officials to provide all relevant documents in the cases it examines, so its recommendations often contain important details—from police, the military, and prosecutors—that are not available elsewhere. The CNDH sends its own medical staff to examine victims or carry out exhumations, providing important first-hand human rights documentation. The commission also produces invaluable resource material, such as the 1998 *Manual For Human Rights Documentation*, published in book and compact disc format, which lists all relevant Mexican and international human rights standards, presented by type of violation.

The National Human Rights Program

On December 21, 1998, the federal government announced the creation of the National Program for the Promotion and Strengthening of Human Rights, an initiative developed jointly by the Ministry of Government, the Foreign Ministry, the Office of the Federal Attorney General, and other government agencies. The initiative was touted as an effort to achieve eight overall goals, including the consolidation of a culture of respect for human rights and of the institutional entities responsible for protecting them, the design of mechanisms to identify positive and negative aspects of Mexican human rights policy, and the dissemination of information about human rights.[13]

The program is positive insofar as it will provide much-needed attention to human rights issues in Mexico. Indeed, the program may aid in the promotion of human rights to the extent that it identifies weaknesses in the government's human rights policies, collects detailed information on cases of human rights violations, reviews Mexican reservations to human rights treaties, and provides human rights education for the public and government employees. In order for the program to be successful, however, authorities will have to develop and implement human rights policies that they have so far failed to produce.

For the most part, the solutions proposed by the program are too vague to permit an analysis of whether or not significant change in Mexican human rights policy will be forthcoming. The program does not appear to establish a well-defined agenda on human rights. It does not provide a diagnosis of the human rights violations that will be the subject of the program—how serious and widespread they are, why they take place, and why prior attempts to resolve them have failed. For the program to succeed, it must have a clearly defined sense of the problem before attempting to resolve it; given that federal authorities have tended to minimize the seriousness of human rights violations in Mexico, it is not clear that such a sense exists or, if it does, that it accurately reflects the true nature of human rights violations in the country. In this regard, detailed consultations with Mexican governmental and nongovernmental human rights organizations would have been valuable but did not take place.

In announcing the initiative, Government Minister Francisco Labastida noted that the government had been working on the program for some four months prior to its launch.[14] Rather than signal the beginning of a process to diagnose Mexico's

---

[13] "Programa Nacional de Promoción y Fortalecimiento de los Derechos Humanos," document sent to Human Rights Watch by Mexico's Foreign Ministry on December 23, 1998, p. 4. The ministries and agencies listed in the program as having taken on human rights commitments are the Ministry of Government, the Mexican Social Security Institute, the Institute of Social Security of Government Employees, the Foreign Ministry, the Ministry of National Defense, the Ministry of the Navy, the Ministry of Public Education, the Ministry of Health, and the Office of the Federal Attorney General.

[14] Foreign Ministry, "Transcripción de las palabras del Licenciado Francisco Labastida Ochoa, Secretario de Gobernación, durante la presentación del Programa Nacional de Promoción y Fortalecimiento de los Derechos Humanos, celebrada en el Salón de Consejos de la Secretaría de Relaciones Exteriores," December 21, 1998.

human rights problems and establish a strategy to address them, however, the program announces human rights initiatives that will be undertaken, such as a national campaign against violence, torture, and impunity. Several key human rights issues are not mentioned, including the military justice system and labor rights. The Ministry of Labor was not even among the ministries involved in developing the program, and it took on no commitments under the initiative. The absence of the Ministry of Labor is a serious oversight, given its strong positions against labor rights taken in the context of NAFTA.[15]

The program notes that its initiatives will be undertaken in coordination with the National Human Rights Commission, provides for periodic review of its success, and solicits input from human rights organizations. It is not clear when or how often such review will take place or the role that nongovernmental human rights groups will play.

---

[15] *See*, for example, Human Rights Watch, "Your Job or Your Rights: Continued Sex Discrimination in Mexico's Maquiladora Sector," *A Human Rights Watch Report*, Vol. 10, No. 1(B), December 1998, pp. 36-41. In response to a case filed under the NAFTA labor side agreement, for instance, the Mexican Labor Ministry has argued that forced pregnancy testing of female job applicants in export-processing zones (*maquiladoras*) does not constitute sex discrimination.

III. HUMAN RIGHTS AND THE JUSTICE SYSTEM IN MEXICO

Mexico's Justice System

More than a legal system, Mexico maintains a legal "thicket," in the words of José Luis Soberanes, director of the Institute of Legal Studies at Mexico's National Autonomous University (Universidad Nacional Autónoma de México, UNAM) until late 1998.[16] Mexico's justice system reflects the federal nature of the country's political system. Each of the country's thirty-one states maintains an independent justice system, while a federal justice system handles federal crimes. In addition, multiple thematic tribunals exist on a federal and, often, a state level; separate tribunals exist for labor conciliation and arbitration, electoral issues, agrarian problems, and military matters, for instance. While each thematic tribunal operates under the jurisdiction of the executive branch, their decisions can be appealed on constitutional grounds to the federal court system.

Federal-jurisdiction crimes include drug trafficking and organized crime and human rights violations committed by federal authorities. Murder, robbery, and kidnapping fall under state jurisdiction.

Mexico's justice system provides for expansive federal-court authority for reviewing the actions of government authorities and laws. The writ of amparo gives federal Mexican courts jurisdiction to entertain any case involving a violation of the Mexican federal constitution through a challenge filed before a federal district court. A challenge could also be made to review a final judgment rendered by a state court that allegedly misapplied state law. The benefit of amparo holds only for the individual case in which the writ was filed.

Since 1984, the federal government has invested in improving the federal system, increasing salaries, modernizing installations, and multiplying the number of courts throughout the country.[17] For instance, Supreme Court legal precedents are available on CD Rom and the Internet, and the federal government compiles statistics on the issues handled by the federal courts.[18] The degree to which state justice systems suffer resource problems varies markedly, but many lag far behind the federal; poor salaries, lack of typewriters and other materials, and a workload that far surpasses the ability of even the most capable judges are the norm.[19] According to *At the Door of the Law*, a book of essays by Mexican lawyers on

---

[16] José Luis Soberanes, "Informe sobre México," in Jorge Correa Sutil, ed., *Situación y políticas judiciales en América Latina* (Santiago, Chile: Universidad Diego Portales, 1993), p. 430.

[17] Héctor Fix Fierro, ed., *A la puerta de la ley: El estado de derecho en México* (México, DF: Cal y Arena, 1994), p. 59.

[18] Ibid., p. 63.

[19] Ibid., p. 60.

problems with the country's legal system, "All indications are that the double system of jurisdictions sharpens the deficiencies of the justice system. On the one hand, this regime does not even fulfill the stated purpose of its existence: that there be local, autonomous justice that is independent of the federal. On the other hand, the autonomy of local justice systems leaves them heterogenous in quality, efficiency, and the way they function in general."[20]

According to the UNAM's Soberanes, if the court system is to function properly, it would first need a major overhaul. In order to get to the heart of the problem, he argues, authorities would have to increase the budget of the state and federal court systems, with more and better-paid judges carrying less burdensome workloads. It would also be necessary to give them better training and to change the way they are named and promoted, in order to guarantee their independence from the executive branch and ensure that their job security did not depend on political caprice.[21] And of course, better training and salaries would also be necessary for prosecutors, police, and public defenders.[22] The overloading of prosecutors, for example, causes serious bottlenecks in Mexico City. While each prosecutor had to resolve sixty-three crimes per year in 1950, that number had gone up to 130 per year in 1980, 140 in 1990, and 219 in 1995,[23] despite an increase in the total number of prosecutors.

---

[20] Ibid., p. 61. Translation by Human Rights Watch.

[21] The Inter-American Commission on Human Rights reported in a September 1998 comprehensive study on human rights in Mexico, "The very constitutional structure of the courts casts doubt on whether they are genuinely independent vis-à-vis the Executive Branch. Indeed, the only members who cannot be removed from office in the entire judicial branch are the justices of the Supreme Court. The fact that circuit magistrates and district judges are subject to transfer until appointed to a new position undermines the principle of genuine unremovability, which is an essential requirement for an independent judicial branch. Moreover, the fact that lower court judges are not unremovable at all, together with the absence of anything that could be called a genuine legal career, gives cause for real concern." The report further notes that Mexico is moving toward the creation of a career service in the judiciary and that some judgeships are now decided by open competition. The report finds, however, that despite the competitions, the Mexican system falls short of establishing a full judicial career service. Inter-American Commission on Human Rights, "Report on the Situation of Human Rights in Mexico," (Washington, DC: Organization of American States, September 24, 1998), OEA/Ser.L/V/II.100, paras. 395 and 398.

[22] Human Rights Watch interview, José Luis Soberanes, Mexico City, June 5, 1998.

[23] Rafael Ruiz Harrell, *Criminalidad y mal gobierno* (Mexico City: Sansores & Aljure, 1998), pp. 66-67.

Investigating Crimes and Prosecuting Criminals

Federal and state-level attorneys general's offices contain what in Mexico is referred to as the "public ministry," which is responsible for the investigation of crimes and prosecution of those responsible, including human rights violators. Through a process known as prior investigation (*averiguación previa*), the prosecutor investigates crimes and identifies the suspect or suspects based on physical evidence and interviews with witnesses, victims, and the accused. Once that is done, the case file is turned over to a judge, who may issue an arrest warrant. If the suspect is arrested in the act of committing a crime, the judge will simply certify that the arrest was legitimate. In either case, the suspect will then give a statement to the judge, known as a preparative statement (*declaración preparatoria*). Based on this information, the judge decides whether or not the prosecution should move forward. If the prosecution is to proceed, the prosecutor's office continues gathering information. There are no jury trials in Mexico, and courts cannot conduct investigations on their own.

Mexico's system of criminal prosecution has been criticized by analysts who maintain that it gives too much authority to prosecutors, who are empowered not only to investigate and obtain evidence but also to validate the evidence they find. According to such critics, prosecutors effectively act as judges, because the results of their actions are accorded the status of proof. That is, they not only seek information, they determine the role it will play in the prosecution. Further, prosecutors take these actions while responsible for prosecuting, not impartially judging the innocence or guilt of the accused.[24] Given the inherently limited scope of this report, Human Rights Watch cannot explore this issue in depth.

Prosecutors are not responsible for investigating crimes alone; they work with judicial police, medical examiners, and other technical experts. In theory, the judicial police take orders from prosecutors, although in practice judicial police often appear to work on their own. Given a long history of abuses by judicial police, successive reforms have limited their authority in the investigative process. Prior to 1984, for instance, judicial police could initiate investigations, but now they may only work on cases assigned to them by prosecutors.[25] Before 1993, statements taken by judicial police were admissible in court. Now only statements made before a prosecutor or judge can be so admitted. Although it was positive that

---

[24] *See* Miguel Sarre, "En busca de un sistema acusatorio," in Jalisco State Human Rights Commission, *Gaceta* 9 (Guadalajara: Comisión Estatal de Derechos Humanos de Jalisco, May-September, 1997), pp. 22-30.

[25] Jorge Garduño Garmendia, *El ministerio público en la investigación de delitos* (México, DF: Noriega Editores, 1991), p. 27.

police lost the authority to take statements that would be admissible as evidence in court, the reform was insufficient; Human Rights Watch believes that only statements made before a judge should be admissible as evidence.

The Public Defender's Office and "Person of Confidence"

Mexico's constitution now ensures that all people subject to investigation or prosecution have the right to be assisted by a lawyer during investigative and trial-related proceedings. If a person cannot afford or does not wish to hire counsel, the court will appoint a public defender.[26] Until 1993, legal defense was guaranteed only during the trial period, not during pre-trial proceedings such as the taking of statements by prosecutors; this was because the constitution only guaranteed the right to *name* a defender for pre-trial proceedings, not to *have* one. Constitutional reforms of 1993 then took precedence over the Supreme Court's ruling that it was up to the detainee to seek a legal defender and that prosecutors could not be held responsible if no lawyer was sought.

Reforms in 1990 created what is called a "person of confidence," an individual trusted by the detainee or declarant who may be present during questioning and other legal processes. If the person of conficence is not a lawyer, a public defender will be named to provide assistance. The suspect may also choose to represent himself or herself.

Even when public defenders are present, the law as written has not always been effective. The chief obstacles to the public defender's work include the large caseload, a lack of professional and non-professional staff, poor training of the lawyers on staff, and corruption, according to people who have studied the system.[27] In several cases documented in this report, public defenders appeared more interested in supporting the prosecution than in aiding their supposed clients. In the Rodríguez Osuna case from Tamaulipas state, for instance, a public defender testified against his alleged client, asserting that his client had voluntarily made a statement to prosecutors with the public defender as counsel, even though the client had retained private counsel and retracted his statement on the grounds that it had been extracted under torture. The judge in the case appeared uninterested in the retraction or alleged irregularities, convicting on the basis of the client's retracted statement.

---

[26] Constitution, Article 20(IX).

[27] National Human Rights Commission, "Proyecto modelo de ley de defensoría de oficio del fuero común" (Mexico City: Comisión Nacional de Derechos Humanos, 1992), p. 8.

The person of confidence is open to the same abuse. In the Soto Miller temporary "disappearance" case, for instance, the victim's two people of confidence actually worked for the prosecutor's office and have failed to appear in court to answer questions about what happened when the victim made his alleged confession.[28] They had not been chosen by Soto Miller. In the García Carrillo case, brought to the attention of Human Rights Watch by the PGR and discussed in the chapter "Impunity and Punishment for Human Rights Violations," police tortured the victim and then provided him with a "person of confidence" who may have had the confidence of the police but did not enjoy the same status with the victim. The prosecutor in the case indicted the victim using the statement he made under such conditions.

Problems with the system of public defenders have been pointed out again and again over the years. In 1992, the CNDH proposed changes to laws regulating state public defenders' offices, noting, "Over the eighteen months of its existence, the National Human Rights Commission has seen many diverse cases that have highlighted a painful reality—that the institution of the public defender does not function as it should. This constitutes a human rights violation in itself, but at the same time is the method through which other constitutional guarantees and prerogatives are violated."[29] Since then, the situation has not improved, as the U.N. special rapporteur on torture found in 1997. "Often victims were unaware that one of the persons around them was in fact a defender, supposedly on his/her side," the U.N. official found. "In brief, the public defender cannot be relied on to defend."[30]

Human Rights Protections Under Mexican Law
Constitutional and procedural guarantees

Article 16 of Mexico's constitution requires that authorities who carry out searches make arrests only with a court order. For an arrest warrant to be issued, the prosecutor who solicits it must show a judge that physical evidence of the crime

---

[28] This problem has been documented by Human Rights Watch in the past. *See* Human Rights Watch/Americas, "Mexico: Torture and Other Abuses During the 1995 Crackdown on Alleged Zapatistas," *A Human Rights Watch Report*, Vol. 8, No. 3(B), February 1996, pp. 13-14.

[29] National Human Rights Commission, "Proyecto Modelo," p. 7. Translation by Human Rights Watch.

[30] United Nations, "Question of the Human Rights of All People Submitted to Any Form of Detention or Imprisonment, in Particular: Torture and Other Cruel, Inhuman or Degrading Treatment or Punishment" (New York: United Nations Publications, January 14, 1998), E/CN.4/1998/38/Add.2, para. 81.

exists, the suspect is linked to the commission of the crime, and information exists that supports the suspect's probable responsibility for the crime. Once the suspect has been arrested, he or she must be placed before a judge "without any delay."[31] There are two exceptions to the need for a judicial order for detention: in case of urgency[32] or when a criminal is caught *in flagrante* or *quasi-in flagrante*.[33] In such cases, a judge must immediately certify that the arrest was legal and, if not, release the detainee.

Article 16 provides that prosecutors, after taking charge of a detainee, have up to forty-eight hours to decide whether to free the suspect or turn him or her over to a judge. Failure to do so constitutes a criminal offense. In cases involving organized crime, the maximum time period is doubled, to ninety-six hours. Other procedural guarantees include the right of suspects or formally accused people to review the evidence against them, provide prosecutors with evidence in their favor, and face and question their accusers. A translator must be provided when needed.

Once a suspect is charged and turned over to a judge, the judge has a maximum of seventy-two hours to move forward with the prosecution or release the detainee, according to Article 19. If the custodial authorities fail to receive orders from the judge within seventy-two hours, the constitution requires them to bring the failure to the attention of the judge. If, three hours after doing so, they do not receive word, they are to release the suspect.

Judges are required to certify the validity of all arrests. In practice, however, cases in which torture and temporary "disappearances" take place are also often accompanied by falsification of police records related to the arrest, and judges in such cases often fail to question suspect or patently false police versions of how detainees came into custody. At the same time, higher courts have ruled that even

---

[31] Constitution, Article 16.

[32] In order to be "urgent," a crime must be "serious" under Mexican law and there must be a "founded risk that the suspect will avoid justice."

[33] Quasi in flagrante includes a suspect who, no longer in the act of committing the crime, is physically pursued by police immediately after doing so, or when the suspect is identified by a third party and then immediately caught with some evidence that would allow the "founded presumption of guilt." Federal Criminal Procedures Code, Article 193. In the Mexico City penal procedural code, this was amended on May 13, 1996, to indicate that such flagrancy would work only within seventy-two hours of a "serious" crime, if no investigation had been begun, and if the investigative pursuit of the crime had not been interrupted. National Human Rights Commission, "Detención arbitraria, inejecución de órdenes de aprehensión y abusos en su cumplimiento," 1996, p. 49.

if lower courts improperly certified arrests, once a judge certifies the indictment, the defendant can be tried.

Article 20 of the constitution provides that no one can be obliged to make a self-incriminating statement to authorities and that any statement made before anyone other than a prosecutor or judge is invalid. It further holds, "All incommunicado detention, intimidation or torture will be punishable under criminal law and is prohibited."

Mexican law also provides for constitutional appeal known in Spanish as amparo. It can be used to challenge the unconstitutional actions of authorities or the constitutionality of laws.

The importance of individual and procedural guarantees

Procedural guarantees related to search, arrest, legal defense, and time periods allotted to police, prosecutors, and judges to carry out their functions serve a fundamental purpose in the protection of human rights. Due process rights, if respected, provide certainty to those subject to police or prosecutorial action about the proceedings underway and those to come. Héctor Faúndez Ledesma, a leading human rights jurist in Latin America, writes of the right to adequate legal representation, "In effect, it is very probable that of all the rights that a person subject to criminal prosecution enjoys, this is the most important, since it permits him to know and exercise fully his other rights."[34] With certainty about the legal process, people subjected to it are much less open to coercion by police or prosecutors. At the same time, procedural guarantees minimize the ability of police or prosecutors to physically or psychologically torture detainees, because they eliminate the amount of time that detainees are unaccounted for.

In Mexico, procedural guarantees take on particular importance, because torture and other serious abuses often follow arbitrary arrest, in which a suspect is detained without court order or other legally founded justification, or prolonged detention, in which the suspect is held in excess of the legally imposed limits. The cases documented in this report conform to this pattern, but it is a practice that has also been well identified by the CNDH. A 1996 commission study of 505 cases found that in more than 30 percent the victim had been arbitrarily detained, and in most of those cases had also been physically mistreated, held incommunicado, or

---

[34] Héctor Faúndez Ledesma, *Administración de justicia y derecho internacional de los derechos humanos* (Caracas: Universidad Central de Venezuela, 1992), p. 310. Translation by Human Rights Watch.

held in detention in excess of the legally defined maximum time.[35] Often, when physical abuse was meted out, the detention coincided with the amount of time the wounds took to heal.[36] When physical violence was used in arbitrary detention cases, the CNDH found, it was usually aimed at obtaining confessions or signatures on blank paper that was later used by authorities to write a confession.[37] Asking for a non-existent search warrant is a good way to get yourself threatened or beaten, according to the CNDH; those responsible for the abuse make a show of mistreating the victim and threatening reprisals if the case is denounced.[38]

The Inter-American Commission on Human Rights has also studied the problem in Mexico. Referring to what it termed the "systematic" problem of illegal detentions in Mexico, the commission determined,

> [T]he most delicate aspect of the problem is that this type of human rights violation often marks the beginning of a chain of violations of other rights, which generally includes the right to personal integrity and legal guarantees. The relationship between illegal detention and the violation of an individual's personal integrity and legal rights is not a function of circumstance. Rather, it is the logical consequence of the relationship of dependency that is often found between the administrative and judicial authorities.[39]

Human Rights Deficiencies in Mexican Law and Legal Precedent

Despite relatively strong constitutional guarantees, Mexican laws and their interpretation have contributed to serious human rights problems. With a few important exceptions, there is no explicit prohibition on the use in court of evidence obtained through human rights violations. The law bars the admission of statements made during torture or made after being held by prosecutors beyond the forty-eight-hour time limit allowed for a decision about whether to indict. At the same time, the law prohibits the use of evidence obtained in violation of the law.

The problem with these standards is that, in practice, they do not lead to the effective exclusion of evidence obtained through human rights violations. Arbitrary

---

[35] National Human Rights Commission, "Procuración de justicia y derechos humanos," 1996, pp. 20 and 40.
[36] Ibid., p. 41.
[37] Ibid., p. 20.
[38] Ibid., p. 39.
[39] Inter-American Commission on Human Rights, "Report on the Situation of Human Rights in Mexico," para. 219.

detention and a detention in excess of the maximum time allowed by law are crimes, at least insofar as they constitute abuse of authority, but they do not necessarily affect the legal status of the detainee once a judge has confirmed the charges. Similarly, illegal arrest and detention do not necessarily constitute grounds for rejecting statements made afterward.

Even after passage of the 1991 Federal Law to Prevent and Punish Torture, motivated in part to ensure that coerced confessions be banned from the legal process, Mexican courts have ruled that confessions given after arbitrary detention are valid as long as the victim admits guilt. The Second Collegiate Court of the Sixth District ruled in 1993, for instance, that even though an arrest had been carried out illegally, the confession made by the victim was valid since he had confessed to the deputy director of investigations of the Office of the Federal Attorney General.[40]

As shown in this report, torture often takes place during illegal detentions; even if a detainee is not tortured at the time of making a statement, torture by police prior to delivery to prosecutors can be just as effective in ensuring that a confession turns out as police desire. Mexican law, however, leaves it up to detainees to prove that their statements were made as a result of the torture they suffered, a tremendously difficult task even if physical evidence of torture exists.

Courts have also ruled that arbitrary arrest does not constitute grounds for releasing the detainee once the detainee has been charged. The Second Collegiate Court of the Sixth District ruled in 1993, for example, that arbitrary arrest "in no way implied that the indictment is unconstitutional." The court based its judgment on the fact that the validity of the indictment depended on the strength of the evidence against the accused and that whether or not the detention was arbitrary would not change the strength of that evidence.[41]

In 1990, the Criminal Procudures Code was reformed to exclude from the judicial process statements made during prolonged detention, a positive change based on the presumption that in such circumstances the authorities involved had tried to coerce the declarant into making a self-incriminating statement.[42] Nonetheless, in order for this prohibition to have any meaning, authorities must be able to clearly establish the details surrounding arrest, including the exact time the

---

[40] *Semanario Judicial de la Federación*, Octava Epoca, Tomo XI, May 1993, p. 308. Available: HTTP://info1.juridicas.unam.mx/jurinfo/penal/PENAL69/PEN34410.HTM [December 14, 1998].

[41] Ibid., p. 322.

[42] Sergio García Ramírez, *Proceso penal y derechos humanos* (Mexico City: Porrúa, 1993) , p. 59.

detainee came into police custody, was turned over to prosecutors, and then handed over to a judge. For their part, judges must insist that such detail is reliably documented. The failure of authorities to offer such detail, or the existence of serious doubts about the veracity of the information provided, should lead to the presumption that the arrest was improper; the presumption should be reversed if authorities prove that no irregularities took place.

Authorities' lack of concern about human rights violations committed during detention and the judicial process undercuts formal human rights protections established in the law. Several cases in this report demonstrate how judges can go out of their way to accept impugned testimonies without addressing the declarant's allegations of torture or inadequate legal defense. Key to their ability to do so is the "principle of procedural immediacy"—the concept in Mexico that the first statement made by a detainee has greater value than later statements.[43] This legal precedent—based on Supreme Court rulings—was cited, for example, in the Rodríguez Osuna case from Tamaulipas state, in which the judge accepted a statement against the defendant made by another man who had apparently been forced into declaring, even though the man had retracted his statement. Serious doubts were also raised about how he had come into detention and about whether he had appropriate legal counsel when he made the statement. Rather than express concern about the alleged coercion, the judge cited procedural immediacy to accept the statement that incriminated Rodríguez Osuna while opting to ignore the retraction because several other pieces of irrelevant evidence were said to support the declarant's initial statement. This legal precedent was also cited in the Soto Miller temporary "disappearance" case, several Oaxaca torture cases, and the Manuel Manríquez torture case, all documented in this report.

Judges have also cited procedural immediacy to reject retractions even when torture is evident. In the case of seven people detained in 1995 in Yanga, Veracruz state, a judge admitted that several of the detainees showed signs of having been beaten. The CNDH eventually issued a recommendation finding that they had been

---

[43] The Mexican use of this concept appears unique. In most countries, the idea of procedural immediacy means that a statement made before a judge can be deemed by that judge to be worthy of more credence than a statement made elsewhere. In fact, the Inter-American Commission on Human Rights has termed the Mexican usage of the term "erroneous." According to the commission, "The Mexican State is construing the [principle of procedural immediacy] in a way which, instead of serving as a procedural guarantee for those accused of a crime, is becoming its very antithesis, the source of abuse of the rights of accused persons." Inter-American Commission on Human Rights, "Report on the Situation of Human Rights in Mexico," paras. 310 and 315.

tortured. Nonetheless, the judge ruled, "The retractions should not be given value on the basis of the alleged unconstitutional acts in which the apprehending agents probably engaged. Given the principle of procedural immediacy, their first depositions are the ones that should take precedence over their later ones, because they were closer to the time of the facts and without sufficient time for thinking about them or electing what to say."[44]

As with confessions or statements, Mexican law does not invalidate physical evidence obtained through human rights violations. Mexico's federal criminal procedures code establishes that evidence obtained through illegal searches cannot be accorded the status of clear proof (*prueba plena*), but it can be used to support other evidence and in sentencing.[45]

Not all Mexican courts disregard human rights concerns in issuing judgements. In fact, some have underscored that violations of procedure invalidate the resulting judicial processes. For instance, the Second Court of the Eighth Circuit ruled that the existence of human rights violations committed during detention do not constitute irreparable acts once a judge has confirmed the indictment of the detainee:

> Even when the lower court has certified the indictment, if the appeals magistrate indicates that Article 16, paragraph six, of the Constitution was violated to the detriment of the detainee, he can and should legally order the release of the detainee, despite the indictment, because the indictment, based on an illegal detention, must also be considered in violation of the Constitution.[46]

Similarly, a judge in 1995 threw out a confession made by a woman who had been illegally detained, arguing that the court had to consider her confession forced if the safeguards in Article 16 of the constitution had not been met.[47] Because of

---

[44] *See* Human Rights Watch/Americas, *Torture and Other Abuses*, p. 17.

[45] Federal Criminal Procedures Code, Article 284.

[46] Segundo Tribunal Colegiado del Octavo Circuito, Amparo en revisión, 314/94. *Semanario Judicial de la Federación*, Octava Época, Tomo XV, January 1995, p. 223. Available: HTTP:/info1.juridicas.unam.mx/jurinfo/penal/PENAL76/PEN37556.HTM. [December 22, 1998.]

[47] *See* Human Rights Watch/Americas, *Torture and Other Abuses*, p. 11. Despite this positive ruling, the woman's confession was used by other courts to convict people she was forced into naming in the confession—another indication of the lack of consistency related to human rights criteria in Mexican courts.

the judge's ruling, the woman was freed. In its response to the Mexico report issued by the Inter-American Commission on Human Rights, the Mexican government presented other court decisions that showed that judges had rejected coerced confessions or that such confessions had been accepted only if additional evidence supported them.[48]

Mexico's justice system, like all others, must balance the goal of discovering the truth in criminal cases with preserving the dignity of those who pass through the system and respecting the rule of law. Indeed, those who drafted Mexico's current constitution argued for clearly demarcating the powers of prosecutors and judges, noting, "During the period since the revolution until now, Mexican judges have been in charge of investigating crimes and seeking evidence, just as in colonial times. To do so, they have always felt authorized to carry out veritable assaults against prisoners in order to get them to confess, which, without a doubt, strips the judiciary of its natural function."[49] From this argument sprang the protections contained in Article 16 of the constitution, which establishes limitations on the circumstances in which police and prosecutors can carry out searches or arrests, limits the amount of time they can hold detainees before turning them over to a judge, and caps the time period judges have to decide whether or not to issue arrest warrants, move forward with prosecutions, and make other decisions related to the fate of detainees.

Mexican jurist Sergio García Ramírez, who is now a judge on the Inter-American Court of Human Rights, has noted,

> In a just state of law, criminal prosecution implies and demands the existence of an effective system of individual guarantees. These guarantees confer legitimacy and rationality on the prosecution, distancing it from a situation in which violence is simply employed over

---

[48] Inter-American Commission on Human Rights, "Report on the Situation of Human Rights in Mexico," paras. 316 and 317. A court unidentified in the report ruled in 1975, "The detention of the accused carried out by police before a complaint had been made implies that the person was coerced and, consequently, the implausibility of the confession." Another court ruled in 1986, "On their own, confessions obtained through prolonged and unjustified detention by police lack probative value. The word of authorities who act arbitrarily also lacks probative value on its own, since it is logical to suppose that the charges they lodge against the detainees are an attempt to justify their arbitrary action."

[49] Cited in National Human Rights Commission, "Detención arbitraria, inejecución de órdenes de aprehensión y abusos en su cumplimiento," Materiales de Trabajo, 1996, p. 21. Translation by Human Rights Watch.

an individual. Without such guarantees we would witness only an unequal confrontation in which force, with no real link to reason, would prevail. In a state of law, the observation of these effective guarantees alone validates the determination of the historical truth, which is the logical purpose of criminal prosecutions. In other words, the search for truth is not an end that justifies the means.[50]

The points made in García Ramírez's somewhat theoretical analysis have also been applied in Mexico, although rarely. The balance between seeking information for prosecution and seeking information at any cost, including the violation of human rights, was the subject of debate in 1990, for instance. At that time, the criminal procedure code was amended to presume that statements made to police during prolonged detentions were coerced and should be ignored. Similarly, the legislative history of Mexico's 1991 Federal Law to Prevent and Punish Torture shows that the Senate commissions that reviewed the law argued that public servants, "whatever their position, should carry out their work in strict accord with the law and, with respect to the investigation of crimes, should seek whatever proof is necessary; but never, under the pretext of seeking the truth, should harm be caused to suspects."[51] The principle underlying these arguments, however, has not been extended to cover other procedural irregularities in Mexico.

Procedural guarantees exist not only in order to provide legal certainty to those in custody and to remove arbitrary authority from police, prosecutors, and judges. They also ensure that procedures used to find evidence, and hence the truth, lead to the discovery of accurate information. If procedural guarantees were scrupulously followed, police and prosecutors would have less opportunity to coerce detainees. If the violation of these procedural safeguards led to a presumption in court that the detainee was coerced, and coercion led to the elimination of the evidence obtained in that manner, police and prosecutors interested in ensuring that evidence held up in court would be forced to adhere to procedural guidelines. There should be no question in the minds of police, prosecutors, and judges that evidence obtained through human rights violations will be thrown out. As part of a federal effort to strengthen the protection of human rights, the government should also promote legislation that would give legal validity only to declarations made before a judge.

---

[50] García Ramírez, *Proceso penal,* pp. 39-40.
[51] Cited in Ibid., p. 343.

Human Rights and the Mexican Justice System

International law recognizes the importance of following procedural safeguards, and establishes guidelines for admissibility of evidence obtained in violation of those guarantees. The United Nations Body of Principles for the Protection of All Persons under Any Form of Detention or Imprisonment includes the need for authorities to record the time at which the detainee was brought into custody and when he or she first appeared before a judge or other judicial authority. It also holds that detainees are entitled to legal counsel. Further, the principles, which form part of the body of international law representing consensus of the international community on such safeguards, establish, "It shall be prohibited to take undue advantage of the situation of a detained or imprisoned person for the purpose of compelling him to confess, to incriminate himself otherwise or to testify against any other person."[52] They continue, "Non-compliance with these principles in obtaining evidence shall be taken into account in determining the admissibility of such evidence against a detained or imprisoned person."[53]

Responsibility for Ensuring the Protection of Human Rights

Mexican law requires that authorities protect human rights and not violate constitutional guarantees, but the Mexican government must do much more to ensure that these standards are observed. While many of the violations documented in this report, like torture, constitute crimes in and of themselves, the negligent response of public officials to those human rights violations also constitutes a breach of the law. Federal prosecutors and judicial police, for instance, are bound to safeguard the "legality" of the process and to "always act in accord with the law and to respect human rights."[54] Violation of this law can lead to suspension or firing. At the same time, Mexican law provides for prison time for "crimes against the administration of justice." It is a crime, for instance, for a public servant to "impede or delay, maliciously or through negligence, the administration of justice" or to "carry out an act or engage in an omission that produces harm or provides someone with an undue advantage.[55] These crimes carry a penalty of between one and six years in prison; Human Rights Watch is aware of several cases in Mexico

---

[52] General Assembly Resolution 43/173, "United Nations Body of Principles for the Protection of All Persons under Any Form of Detention or Imprisonment," December 9, 1988, Principles 12, 17, and 21.

[53] Ibid., Principle 27.

[54] Basic Law of the Office of the Federal Attorney General (Ley Orgánica de la Procuraduría General de la República), Article 51(I).

[55] Penal Code, Article 225(VIII and VII).

in which charges were brought against a federal prosecutor using this provision of the penal code.

In certain cases, including torture, prosecutors are required to open investigations with or without a complaint from the victim. However, even in cases that require a complaint to be filed, if a prosecutor learns of an abuse, he or she is required to bring it to the attention of the victim.[56] The victim could press charges, then. The prosecutor's failure to raise the issue with the victim, therefore, constitutes a failure to live up to the administrative requirements of the job and could constitute a crime against the administration of justice.

Judicial Reforms in Mexico

Any discussion of judicial reforms in Mexico must begin with a distinction between the law as written, the law as applied, and the law as interpreted by the courts. Indeed, Mexico has a long tradition of incorporating broad human rights protections in its constitutions.[57] But constitutional human rights protections have not been consistently enforced. "The great theme of our constitutional history has been the separation, if not abyss, between standards and reality, the almost congenital inability of the former to significantly modify the latter,"[58] according to *At the Door of the Law*.

José Luis Soberanes of the UNAM has bluntly noted the difficulty in promoting effective legal reforms in Mexico, highlighting at the same time the importance of undertaking effective reforms: "In effect, delivery of justice in Mexico depends on a structure that is complicated, slippery, and often corrupt. It seems unreformable because the foremost enemies of change are the very judicial functionaries who are ready to fight for the defense of their antiquated and poorly functioning judicial system and, yes, their privileges and sinecures."[59] Mexican legal experts have also criticized some judicial reforms as motivated more by political expedience than by need.[60]

---

[56] Basic Law of the Office of the Federal Attorney General, Article 8(I).

[57] Fix Fierro, ed., *A la puerta de la ley*, p. 17.

[58] Ibid. Translation by Human Rights Watch.

[59] José Luis Soberanes, "Informe sobre México," p. 429. Translation by Human Rights Watch.

[60] Judicial reforms carried out in 1994 and 1995, for instance, followed campaign promises made by Ernesto Zedillo when he was a presidential candidate. They were submitted to Congress just days after he became president and were approved only ten days later after no public debate. *See* Sergio García Ramírez, *Poder judicial y ministerio público* (Mexico City: Porrúa, 1997), pp. 41-44.

Human Rights and the Mexican Justice System

Reforms this decade have focused on both improving human rights guarantees and improving the efficiency of police work, goals that in Mexico have often, though unnecessarily, been at odds. Without doubt, the need to improve the work of police and prosecutors is great. Indeed, in 1995, only 2.5 percent of the 218,599 crimes reported in Mexico City resulted in the indictment of a suspect.[61] Compared with major cities such as Paris, Rome, London, Madrid, Rio de Janeiro, Sâo Paulo, and New York, Mexico City registers the worst crime-resolution rate.[62] The argument often made by authorities to justify this poor showing is that the nature of crime has changed, while laws have not.[63] Rafael Ruiz Harrell, a critic of this justification, summarizes the official view as follows: "If we want to reduce the level of impunity it is necessary, therefore, to update the law, strengthen sanctions, and limit cases that allow release on bail. Above all else, it is imperative to establish more elastic terms for police action—and restrict suspects' guarantees."[64] From a human rights standpoint, this approach is troubling because it leads to greater limitations on individual guarantees; when a central problem in human rights cases in Mexico is the violation of individual guarantees leading to torture, "disappearance," or extrajudicial execution, greater, not weaker, protections should be sought. The fight against crime in Mexico, dubbed the "National Crusade against Crime," cannot justify violating or restricting human rights.

To analyze all aspects of the legal reforms that have taken place in Mexico in recent years is beyond the scope of this report. We focus instead on the most salient issues relevant to individual guarantees and impunity. In 1990, 1993, 1994-1995, and 1996 legal reforms were enacted, some of which strengthened and some of which weakened human rights protections.[65] The 1990 reforms were focused expressly on strengthening human rights protections, invalidating statements made by detainees if they were held beyond legally mandated limits and giving the National Human Rights Commission authority to solicit information from public officials, for instance.[66] Other positive changes followed. For instance, Article 20

---

[61] Ruiz Harrell, *Criminalidad y mal gobierno*, p. 61.
[62] Ibid., p. 64.
[63] Ibid., p. 62.
[64] Ibid.
[65] Part of this chapter draws on an article published by the author in June 1998. *See* Joel Solomon, "Derechos humanos y combate a la delincuencia," *La Jornada* (Mexico City), June 28, 1998.
[66] For a full discussion of the 1990 reforms, *see* García Ramírez, *Proceso penal.* The provision that statements made to police are invalid if made during a detention that exceeded the maximum time limit was based on the supposition that police tried to pressure the

of the constitution was amended in 1993 so that detainees' statements to police would lack legal value as evidence in criminal cases, an important step toward stripping police of one of their strongest justifications for torturing detainees. In practice, police do not now take statements from detainees to be used in court. As positive as this change has been, though, police are still able to coerce detainees by threatening or torturing them prior to their issuance of official declarations. Nonetheless, statements taken by prosecutors have been shown to have serious problems as well, leading to the conclusion that only statements made before a judge should be accepted in court.

The prohibition in court of statements taken by police was one in a series designed to reduce the prevalence of torture; others included establishing criminal penalties for prosecutors who failed to ensure that detainees were represented by a legal defender during pre-trial proceedings and clarification of time limits for prosecutors to bring detainees to a judge.[67] Similarly, after Article 21 of the constitution was reformed in 1994, victims could challenge the decision by prosecutors not to press charges against alleged criminals, including human rights violators, although at this writing authorities had yet to pass a law that would implement this constitutional right.[68]

During 1993 and 1994, however, additional constitutional reforms came into effect that limit individual guarantees. For instance, prosecutors were given the authority to carry out arrests in certain cases without a court order, even if the

---

detainee into incriminating him or herself.

[67] For a detailed analysis of the anti-torture reforms, *see* Luis de la Barreda Solórzano, *La lid contra la tortura* (Mexico City: Cal y Arena, 1995).

[68] A debate exists in Mexico about whether the proper way for this right to be exercised is through specific legislation or through the process of constitutional challenge known as amparo. The Inter-American Commission on Human Rights has welcomed the constitution's recognition of the right to challenge a prosecutor's decision not to prosecute, but has strongly criticized Mexico for failing to take the steps necessary to ensure that this right can be exercised simply, swiftly, and effectively. Although Mexico's Supreme Court has held that a prosecutor's decision not to prosecute can be subject to amparo, the commission has deemed this step positive but insufficient, because the ruling did not create obligatory legal precedent. The commission has recommended to the Mexican government that it regulate Article 21 of the constitution with a specific law. See Inter-American Commission on Human Rights, Report No. 48/97, Case 11.520, February 18, 1998, reprinted in Inter-American Commission on Human Rights, *Annual Report of the Inter-American Commission on Human Rights* (Washington, DC: Organization of American States, 1998), pp. 681-91.

suspect was not caught in the act.[69] This authority, according to jurist Ignacio Burgoa, "opens the door to unlimited subjective actions by administrative authorities... to limit personal liberties."[70] July 1996 reforms to Articles 16, 20, and 22 of the constitution gave broader power to prosecutors to fight crime, including phone-tapping, expanded authority to request that judges deny bail, and a wider range of instances in which they can confiscate goods.[71] Later that year, the Law to Fight Organized Crime entered into force, doubling the time prosecutors can hold suspects before turning them over to a judge—from forty-eight to ninety-six hours.

Soon after becoming president in 1994, Ernesto Zedillo proposed structural reforms to Mexico's court system, including modifications to the Supreme Court and the creation of a Federal Judicial Council, responsible for the administration of the courts and oversight, discipline, and naming of judges. Following the reforms, the number of Supreme Court justices dropped from twenty-six to eleven, and their appointment must be confirmed by the Senate. "This [structural reform] may prove important for the future independence of the court," according to Beatriz Magaloni, a lawyer who has worked on human rights issues, "particularly in consideration of the growing strength of opposition parties and the likelihood of a more effective system of checks and balances."[72] The Federal Judicial Council may help to professionalize the judiciary and could potentially play an important role in promoting human rights by overseeing the work of judges with respect to human rights issues. The councils could document cases in which judges accept evidence obtained through human rights violations or otherwise fail to ensure that procedural or individual guarantees were observed throughout the legal processes in cases that come before them. Appropriate administrative or criminal punishment could be pursued against judges when such cases occur.

---

[69] Prosecutors can make such arrests "Only in urgent cases, when the matter relates to a serious crime as defined by law, and when there is a founded risk that the suspect could flee from the law, and only if the prosecutor cannot get to a judge. . . ." Translation by Human Rights Watch.

[70] Ignacio Burgoa, *Las garantías indivduales* (Mexico City: Editorial Porrúa, 1996), p. 621.

[71] Mariclaire Acosta, "El caso mexicano: otra vuelta de tuerca," Comisión Mexicana de Defensa y Promoción de los Derechos Humanos, March 1997, p. 4.

[72] Beatriz Magaloni, "Judicial Reform Starts at the Top," *Los Angeles Times*, July 25, 1997. Nonetheless, in certain circumstances the president may simply name Supreme Court justices; if the Senate twice rejects the president's list of three candidates, the president can fill the position unilaterally.

No matter how successful structural reforms may ultimately be, however, they alone would not resolve the underlying human rights problems inherent in the Mexican justice system. As García Ramírez has suggested, the changes that took place in 1994 were "macro," rather than "micro" reforms, far from the sphere in which the majority of incidents and interactions that influence the administration of justice take place. Rather, he has argued, the area in which the day-to-day problems of millions of individuals are laid out and resolved ". . . is made up of the sum of the organs, procedures, and measures that take place on the lower rungs of system: police offices, prosecutors' offices, courts belonging to justices of the peace, trial-level courts, the specialized thematic courts (labor, administrative, agrarian, children), etc."[73]

In December 1997, President Zedillo sent new proposed legal reforms to the Senate. Behind the proposals lies the fallacy that "certain legal requisites, developed in their context to confront a criminality lacking in the sophistication that is evident today, limit the ability of authorities to act."[74] In essence, President Zedillo argued that human rights guarantees constitute a straitjacket in the fight against increasingly sophisticated crime.

Among the most questionable proposed reforms were changes in the requirements for obtaining an arrest warrant and for a judge to jail an indicted suspect. If finally approved, the reforms would make it much easier for suspects to be jailed on weaker evidence and without certainty that a crime had even been committed. The attorney general of Mexico has explained that the reforms are an attempt to "define, clarify, and make more precise the responsibilities of the judges and the responsibilities of the prosecutors within the realm of criminal procedure," and that they are aimed at harmonizing "due process-related guarantees with repairing the harm done to victims and with society's legitimate interest in punishing criminals that have harmed and offended it."[75] However, the reforms would open the door even wider to all kinds of abuse already prevalent in the justice system. They would increase the chances that an innocent person would be subjected to unjust prosecution, which is particularly serious given Mexico's weak public defender's office.

---

[73] García Ramírez, *Poder judicial y ministerio público*, pp. 34-35.

[74] Ernesto Zedillo, "Iniciativa de reforma a los artículos 16, 19, 20, 22 y 123, Apartado B, fracción XIII, de la Constitución Política de los Estados Unidos Mexicanos," December 3, 1997, p. 2. Translation by Human Rights Watch.

[75] Jorge Madrazo, speech on the proposed law, December 7, 1997, provided to Human Rights Watch by the Office of the Federal Attorney General.

According to an analysis by the Citizens' Legislative Proposal Workshop, a group of jurists and human rights experts, ". . . it would be wrong to believe that the way to resolve the very serious and intolerable problem of public insecurity . . . is precisely to create a new cause for public insecurity, which is what would result from reducing through these reforms constitutional guarantees that protect citizens in general from authorities. [Similarly, insecurity would result from] giving authorities more discretionary power, which would allow them to limit these guarantees more easily."[76] Mireille Roccatti, president of the CNDH, told Human Rights Watch the same thing in different words. "We'd be creating a monster," she warned, since "the authorities are often the very ones responsible for [criminal acts]."[77]

To accompany the legal reforms, the government developed what it called "Strategies and Actions of the National Public Security Program," which consist of eight focal points for attention from federal and state authorities. Training, testing, hiring more law enforcement and court personnel, and establishing centralized data bases were among the steps promised by the government.[78] Funding would be increased to reach these goals. Several of the proposals to fight crime, such as creation of new nationwide data bases and expanding citizen participation in oversight of police, would lend themselves to the protection of human rights.

Unfortunately, human rights violations were not included in the problems to be addressed by these programs, and the strategies announced by the government did not make any reference to improving the way authorities monitor or respond to human rights abuses. In fact, expanding personnel without attending to underlying human rights concerns may worsen human rights problems. An explicit human rights focus should be an integral part of any government strategy designed to address public security problems.

After announcing its strategies for fighting crime, the federal government said it would create a new police force, called Federal Preventive Police, designed to prevent crimes of a federal nature and to assist federal judicial police in carrying out investigations. Before moving forward with the creation of a new police force,

---

[76] Citizens' Workshop on Legislative Proposals (Taller Ciudadano de Propuesta Legislativa), "Las reformas constitucionales en materia penal, irrelevantes para el restablecimiento de la seguridad pública," no date, p. 1. Translation by Human Rights Watch.

[77] Human Rights Watch interview, Mireille Roccatti, Mexico City, June 8, 1998.

[78] Government Ministry, "Estrategias y Acciones del Programa Nacional de Seguridad Pública: Los Ocho Ejes," November 16, 1998.

the government should publicly provide a clear strategy for ensuring that human rights violations committed by these officers will be investigated and that the offending authorities will be prosecuted. The new police force offers an opportunity to include, from the outset, mechanisms to enhance the protection and promotion of human rights.

IV. MEXICO'S INTERNATIONAL HUMAN RIGHTS OBLIGATIONS

Mexico is bound by human rights treaties violated repeatedly in the cases documented in this report.[79] In addition, these cases highlight the frequent disregard for other, non-binding international standards regarding actions and use of force by police, which represent the international community's statement of adequate treatment of detainees and suspects by authorities.

The Mexican government has rejected Human Rights Watch's use of international standards to analyze human rights practices in Mexico, arguing that "unilateral reports"—those produced outside the framework of an international body like the United Nations—lack "legal value" and "minimize the value of international law."[80] However, Mexico is legally bound by the human rights treaties it has ratified; to suggest that it is wrong for any group or observer to point out how and when Mexico fails to live up to these obligations is simply to seek an excuse for noncompliance.

Torture

Mexico has ratified two treaties that focus exclusively on the prohibition of torture and two others that include express prohibitions against this human rights violation.[81] Authorities are responsible for fully investigating allegations of torture *and any situation in which there is reasonable ground to believe torture may have taken place*, even if the victim does not explicitly allege to have suffered torture.[82] The failure to investigate and to act on the findings of the investigation constitutes a violation of specific provisions of international law. Torturers must be brought to justice. Further, statements given under conditions of torture or cruel and

---

[79] The country's constitution gives ratified treaties the status of domestic law. Article 133 of the constitution holds, "This Constitution, the laws of Congress based on it, and all treaties in accord with it. . .will be the supreme law of the Union." Translation by Human Rights Watch.

[80] This approach was used in a press release issued by Mexico's Foreign Ministry on April 29, 1997, in response to the Human Rights Watch report *Implausible Deniability: State Responsibility for Rural Violence in Mexico*, published in April 1997.

[81] Convention against Torture and Other Cruel, Inhuman, or Degrading Treatment or Punishment, ratified by Mexico on January 23, 1986; Inter-American Convention to Prevent and Punish Torture, ratified by Mexico on June 22, 1987. Torture is also prohibited under: Article 7 of the International Covenant on Civil and Political Rights, ratified by Mexico on March 23, 1981; and Article 5 of the American Convention on Human Rights, ratified by Mexico on March 24, 1981.

[82] Convention against Torture and Other Cruel, Inhuman, or Degrading Treatment or Punishment, Articles 12 and 13; Inter-American Convention to Prevent and Punish Torture, Article 8.

unusual punishment cannot be used as evidence.[83] Prosecutors and judges have the responsibility to investigate any reasonable ground of torture. Prior to using the statement of a suspected torture victim, a prosecutor would have to establish that the statement was not made in circumstances defined as torture by international law.[84]

Torture is not only a heinous act and very serious crime. The abuse when linked to the judicial process may distort proceedings long after the act took place. A detainee tortured by police then turned over to a civilian prosecutor may, with good reason, testify as the police ordered out of fear of being tortured further, even if the victim never sees the officers again. For these reasons, judges must take extremely seriously their responsibility to ensure that any act of torture documented or suspected or alleged to have taken place is investigated. A judge who cites Mexican legal precedent that permits clearly torture-induced statements to be used in court violates provisions of binding international law; likewise, under binding international standards, judges cannot accept evidence if there are reasonable grounds for suspecting that it was obtained through torture.

Mexico is also required to ensure that torture is punishable under its laws. The Federal Law to Prevent and Punish Torture establishes a solid domestic standard to fight torture, and most Mexican states have similar laws on the books. The law, however, is not rigorously enforced. Torturers, if charged at all, may be accused of a lesser crime, such as "abuse of authority."

"Disappearance"

"Disappearances" take place when a state agent—or a person acting with official authorization, support, or acquiescence—deprives someone of liberty without providing information about the detention, or denies having that person in

---

[83] Convention against Torture and Other Cruel, Inhuman, or Degrading Treatment or Punishment, Articles 15; Inter-American Convention to Prevent and Punish Torture, Article 10.

[84] Article 1(1) of the Convention against Torture and Other Cruel, Inhuman, or Degrading Treatment or Punishment provides a standard definition of torture: "For the purposes of this Convention, the term 'torture' means any act by which severe pain or suffering, whether physical or mental, is intentionally inflicted on a person for such purposes as obtaining from him or a third person information or a confession, punishing him for an act he or a third person has committed or is suspected of having committed, or intimidating or coercing him or a third person, or for any reason based on discrimination of any kind, when such pain or suffering is inflicted by or at the instigation of or with the consent or acquiescence of a public official or the person acting in an official capacity."

custody, thereby rendering ineffective all legal remedies or judicial guarantees that might otherwise have protected the victim.[85]

When such abuses take place, multiple violations of international human rights standards occur, including the right to judicial protection and the right to personal liberty. Often, such cases also involve torture and the violation of the right to life. As the Inter-American Court of Human Rights has found,

> The forced disappearance of human beings is a multiple and continuous violation of many rights under the [American Convention on Human Rights] that the States Parties are obligated to respect and guarantee. The kidnapping of a person is an arbitrary deprivation of liberty, an infringement of a detainee's right to be taken without delay before a judge and to invoke the appropriate procedures to review the legality of the arrest. . . . Moreover, prolonged isolation and deprivation of communication are in themselves cruel and inhuman treatment, harmful to the psychological and moral integrity of the person. . . . In addition, investigations into the practice of disappearances and the testimony of victims who have regained their liberty show that those who are disappeared are often subjected to merciless treatment, including all types of indignities, torture, and other cruel, inhuman and degrading treatment. . . .[86]

The U.N. Declaration on the Protection of All Persons from Enforced Disappearance notes that the practice undermines "the deepest values of any society committed to respect for the rule of law, human rights and fundamental freedoms, and that the systematic practice of such acts is of the nature of a crime

---

[85] The United Nations Declaration on the Protection of all Persons from Enforced Disappearance, approved by General Assembly resolution 47/133 of December 18, 1992, describes in more detail that "disappearances" take place when "persons are arrested, detained or abducted against their will or otherwise deprived of their liberty by officials of different branches or levels of Government, or by organized groups or private individuals acting on behalf of, or with the support, direct or indirect, consent or acquiescence of the Government, followed by a refusal to disclose the fate or whereabouts of the persons concerned or a refusal to acknowledge the deprivation of their liberty, which places such persons outside the protection of the law."

[86] Inter-American Court of Human Rights, Velásquez Rodríguez Case, Judgment of July 29, 1988, Inter-Am.Ct.H.R., (Ser. C) No. 4 (1988), paras. 155 and 156.

against humanity. . . ."⁸⁷ The declaration further urges, "Each State shall take effective legislative, administrative, judicial or other measures to prevent and terminate acts of enforced disappearance in any territory under its jurisdiction."⁸⁸ Mexico's penal code does not criminalize "disappearances," although the CNDH has drafted a legal proposal to codify the crime.⁸⁹

In eight years of existence, the CNDH has received more than 1,100 complaints of "disappearances" that reportedly took place since 1969. In these cases, 209 people have been found alive, and ninety-eight others have been found dead. The number of reported cases surged between 1974 and 1978, when guerrilla movements in Mexico grew, and again after 1994, when guerrilla movements and drug trafficking gained momentum.⁹⁰

Extrajudicial Execution

Extrajudicial executions occur when a public authority arbitrarily and deliberately takes the life of a human being in circumstances other than those related to the legitimate use of force in situations such as may occur in an armed confrontation or in carrying out the death penalty.⁹¹ Executions of this type are also considered to have taken place when public officials tolerate or acquiesce to killings by nongovernmental actors. International law clearly prohibits extrajudicial executions as a violation of the right to life.⁹²

Several cases analyzed in this report include extrajudicial execution. In such cases it is common for authorities to assert that the victim committed suicide, or died in an armed confrontation. For example, in the case of Celerino Jiménez

---

⁸⁷ Declaration on the Protection of All Persons from Enforced Disappearance, G.A. res. 47/133, 47 U.N. GAOR Supp. (No. 49) at 207, U.N. Doc. A/47/49 (1992). Adopted by General Assembly resolution 47/133 of December 18, 1992.

⁸⁸ Declaration on the Protection of All Persons from Enforced Disappearance, Article 3.

⁸⁹ National Human Rights Commission, "Anteproyecto de Tipo Penal de Desaparición Forzada o Involuntaria de Personas," no date.

⁹⁰ National Human Rights Commission, *Informe anual de actividades mayo 1997-mayo 1998* (Mexico DF: Comisión Nacional de Derechos Humanos, 1998), p. 751.

⁹¹ Human Rights Watch opposes the use of the death penalty in any circumstances, given the inherently arbitrary nature of its application and the cruelty of the punishment. However, even given this opposition, we must conceptually distinguish the death penalty, applied after a judicial proceeding, from the taking of life without a proper judicial decision.

⁹² Article 6 of the International Covenant on Civil and Political Rights holds that "No one shall be arbitrarily deprived of his life." Article 4 of the American Convention on Human Rights establishes a similar guarantee.

Almaraz, documented in the chapter on Oaxaca state, authorities insist that the victim died in a shoot-out, even though medical evidence suggests that he was shot at close range. In the Cárdenas Esqueda case, analyzed in the Tamaulipas chapter, authorities insisted that the victim killed himself.

Violations of Procedural Guarantees

Due process guarantees are essential for the proper functioning of any judicial system. International law requires that criminal suspects, whether or not they are in detention, benefit from procedural guarantees that ensure that the process is fair.[93] Chief among these guarantees is the right to an adequate legal defense. International law also establishes procedural guarantees related to arrest and detention and prompt access to a judge once an individual has been charged with a crime.[94]

The violation of procedural guarantees also frequently takes place in Mexico in the form of illegal detentions or searches, prolonged detentions, and the falsification of evidence. The torture, "disappearance," and extrajudicial execution cases documented in this report were often accompanied by overt or suspected violations of this nature. Violations of these guarantees facilitate torture by limiting opportunities for establishing accountability and restricting the victims' access to safeguards, like access to a defense lawyer.

Responsibility to Ensure the Full Exercise of Human Rights and an Effective Remedy for Violations

The Mexican government is obliged under international law to ensure that all people under its jurisdiction are able to exercise their human rights.[95] Federal authorities, therefore, are required to take action when they learn of human rights violations. When officials deny that violations occur, as often happened in cases

---

[93] International Covenant on Civil and Political Rights, Article 14 and American Convention on Human Rights, Article 8.

[94] International Covenant on Civil and Political Rights, Article 9 and American Convention on Human Rights, Article 8.

[95] Article 1(1) of the American Convention on Human Rights holds, "The States Parties to this Convention undertake to respect the rights and freedoms recognized herein and to ensure to all persons subject to their jurisdiction the free and full exercise of those rights and freedoms, without any discrimination for reasons of race, color, sex, language, religion, political or other opinion, national or social origin, economic status, birth, or any other social condition." Article 2(1) of the International Covenant on Civil and Political Rights contains substantially similar wording.

documented in this report, or sit back passively as violations take place, such as they did in Morelos state, as described below, they violate this obligation. Although Mexican law provides the amparo mechanism to challenge arbitrary acts by government officials and to obtain a court order for authorities to present someone who has been detained, the mechanism fails to function effectively in "disappearance" cases. The existence of a procedure is not enough to satisfy its obligations under international law; the procedure must also be effective.

In a ground-breaking legal decision, the Inter-American Court of Human Rights interpreted the American Convention on Human Rights to require governments to take affirmative action toward this end, including measures to prevent human rights violations:

> This obligation implies the duty of the States Parties to organize the governmental apparatus and, in general, all the structures through which public power is exercised, so that they are capable of juridically ensuring the free and full enjoyment of human rights. As a consequence of this obligation, the States must prevent, investigate and punish any violation of the rights recognized by the Convention and, moreover, if possible attempt to restore the right violated and provide compensation as warranted for damages resulting from the violation.[96]

It is not enough for authorities to pass laws protective of human rights and establish formal structures to implement them. The state can be held liable under international law for human rights violations, including "disappearances," when judicial mechanisms are ineffective for resolving these problems. According to the court, "The obligation to ensure the free and full exercise of human rights is not fulfilled by the existence of a legal system designed to make it possible to comply with this obligation—it also requires the government to conduct itself so as to effectively ensure the free and full exercise of human rights."[97] The passage of the 1991 Federal Law to Prevent and Punish Torture was important, but, by failing to implement effective policies to eradicate torture, it is insufficient by itself to bring Mexico into compliance with international human rights standards.

---

[96] Inter-American Court of Human Rights, Velásquez Rodríguez judgement of 1988, para. 166.

[97] Ibid., para. 167.

Authorities must also ensure that victims of human rights violations have an effective remedy for the violation suffered.[98] Impunity for human rights violations, therefore, is not simply an added insult and injury to the victim, it is in itself a violation of human rights standards. Torture must be investigated by authorities whether or not the victim files a formal complaint. In the Rodríguez Tapia case in Baja California, described below, for example, federal authorities acted in consonance with this requirement after a man was tortured to death by federal police in Baja California state in 1997. Within months, the police officer had been investigated, indicted, and jailed.

Rehabilitation for and Compensation to Victims of Violations

International human rights law requires governments whose agents engage in serious human rights violations to compensate the victims. The Convention against Torture and Other Cruel, Inhuman, or Degrading Treatment or Punishment, for instance, requires governments to ensure an enforceable right to fair and adequate compensation, including the means for as full a rehabilitation as possible; if a torture victims dies as a result of the torture he or she suffered, the victim's dependents also have a right to compensation.[99] The American Convention on Human Rights establishes the right to compensation for any person sentenced by a final judgement through a miscarriage of justice,[100] and the Inter-American Court of Human Rights has authority to order governments to pay damages in cases in which it determines that rights protected by the convention were violated.[101] The court has used this authority, for instance, in cases of "disappearance."[102]

The International Covenant on Civil and Political Rights holds that any victim of unlawful arrest or detention shall have an enforceable right to compensation.[103] However, when Mexico ratified the covenant, it issued a reservation to the article

---

[98] International Covenant on Civil and Political Rights, Article 2(3) and American Convention on Human Rights, Article 25.

[99] Convention against Torture and Other Cruel, Inhuman, or Degrading Treatment or Punishment, Article 14(1).

[100] American Convention on Human Rights, Article 10.

[101] American Convention on Human Rights, Article 63(1).

[102] See, for instance, Inter-American Court of Human Rights, Godínez Cruz Case, Compensatory Damages, Judgment of July 21, 1989, Inter-Am.Ct.H.R. (Ser. C) No. 8 (1990) and Inter-American Court of Human Rights, Velásquez Rodríguez Case, Compensatory Damages, Judgment of July 21, 1989, Inter-Am.Ct.H.R. (Ser. C) No. 7 (1990).

[103] International Covenant on Civil and Political Rights, Article 9(5).

that establishes this guarantee. Asserting that Mexico's constitution and laws guarantee due process rights, the Mexican government argued that reparations would only be made in cases in which wrongful detentions resulted from a false denunciation or complaint.[104] Mexico's National Human Rights Commission criticized the limitation contained in the reservation. Noting that illegal detentions are the "daily bread of our country" and that they stem from so many illegitimate causes, "reparations should not be limited only to cases that come from 'falsehood in the denunciation or complaint.'"[105]

International Standards on Police Actions and Use of Force

In addition to binding treaties that bear on the actions and use of force by police, the United Nations has developed detailed principles, minimum rules, and declarations on the subject. Taken together, both sources of standards "offer a comprehensive and detailed international legal framework for ensuring respect for human rights, freedom and dignity in the context of criminal justice," according to the United Nations' Centre for Human Rights.[106]

There can be no doubt that arbitrary and physically abusive actions by police violate international human rights standards. As described above, the International Covenant on Civil and Political Rights and the American Convention on Human Rights prohibit the arbitrary searches, detentions, and arrests that are commonplace in Mexico, as well as torture and other mistreatment committed by police officers. At the same time, the U.N. Code of Conduct for Law Enforcement Officials expressly limits the use of force by police to situations in which it is "strictly necessary and to the extent required for the performance of their duty."[107] Although the code is not binding international law, it constitutes authoritative guidance for interpreting international human rights law regarding policing.

Similarly, the U.N.'s Basic Principles on the Use of Force and Firearms by Law Enforcement Officials holds, "Law enforcement officials, in carrying out their duty, shall, as far as possible, apply non-violent means before resorting to the use of force and firearms. They may use force and firearms only if other means remain

---

[104] National Human Rights Commission, *Las reservas formuladas por México a instrumentos internacionales sobre derechos humanos* (Mexico City: Comisión Nacional de Derechos Humanos, 1996), p. 62.

[105] Ibid., pp. 67-68.

[106] Centre for Human Rights, *Human Rights and Law Enforcement* (New York: United Nations, 1997), pp. 25-26.

[107] Code of Conduct for Law Enforcement Officials, Article 3.

ineffective or without any promise of achieving the intended result."[108] Firearms may only be used in very specific circumstances, according to the principles: "Law enforcement officials shall not use firearms against persons except in self-defence or defence of others against the imminent threat of death or serious injury [or] to prevent the perpetration of a particularly serious crime involving grave threat to life. . . ."[109]

Federal Responsibility for Violations by State or Local Authorities

Mexico's federal government is responsible for ensuring that all people in the country or subject to its jurisdiction can freely exercise the human rights defined by the treaties to which it is party. In federal systems of government like Mexico's, the central government cannot avoid its international human rights responsibilities by claiming an abuse was committed by a state-level authority, not a federal official; a hands-off approach to such cases would violate both hemispheric and world-wide standards.[110] Given that one of the federal government's international human rights obligations involves ensuring that human rights can be enjoyed, the government has the affirmative obligation to make sure that state police, prosecutors, and judges act in accord with the human rights principles found in international law.

In order for Mexico to fulfill its obligations under international law, the government must develop effective mechanisms for taking action on serious human rights violations committed by state- or municipal-level officials, even when no federal authority was directly involved in the commission of the abuse. Torture, "disappearance," extrajudicial execution, and grossly abusive arbitrary detention that lead to violations of the right to life or physical integrity should be among the human rights violations subject to obligatory federal jurisdiction. Currently, only torture is covered under a federal law, but the law only gives federal officials

---

[108] Basic Principles on the Use of Force and Firearms by Law Enforcement Officials, General Provision 4.

[109] Ibid., General Provision 9.

[110] Article 28 of the American Convention on Human Rights holds, "With respect to the provisions over whose subject matter the constituent units of the federal state have jurisdiction, the national government shall immediately take suitable measures, in accordance with its constitution and its laws, to the end that the competent authorities of the constituent units may adopt appropriate provisions for the fulfillment of this Convention." Article 50 of the International Covenant on Civil and Political Rights reads, "The provisions of the present Covenant shall extend to all parts of the federal States without any limitations or exceptions."

responsibility for handling cases of torture committed by federal agents. Just as certain crimes already fall under federal jurisdiction regardless of who commits the offense or where it takes place—including drug trafficking and other organized criminal enterprises—serious human rights violations should be designated federal crimes regardless of the agent who commits them. By clarifying which authorities are responsible for resolving these human rights cases and eliminating the need for thirty-one separate state jurisdictions to make appropriate reforms as a prerequisite to resolving them, federal authorities would be in a better position to fulfill their international obligation to ensure that human rights violations are properly resolved throughout the country. Federal attention to these crimes should not come at the expense of strengthening state justice systems.

Human rights violations other than torture, "disappearance," extrajudicial execution, and grossly abusive arbitrary detention that lead to violations of the right to life or physical integrity should also come under federal jurisdiction when a systematic or widespread practice of such violations takes place and when state governments fail to prosecute them.

V. TORTURE AND EXTRAJUDICIAL EXECUTION IN TAMAULIPAS STATE

Tamaulipas state, on the northern border with the United States, demonstrates the complexity of human rights problems in Mexico. Abuses there do not stem from the armed conflicts present in southern Mexico, yet arbitrary detention, torture, and extrajudicial execution take place. Both state and federal authorities demonstrate a lack of interest in ensuring that detainees benefit from fair judicial processes and that human rights violators are brought to justice. When questioned on the patently false information used to prosecute Juan Lorenzo Rodríguez Osuna, for instance, the state attorney general told Human Rights Watch, "I would be remiss in my duties if I didn't prosecute him."[111] It is a sad irony of the cases reviewed here that the victims of human rights violations were more often successfully prosecuted than the human rights violators.

The recent cases described below are not isolated. They clearly conform to a pattern documented for at least a decade by the Tamaulipas-based Center for Border Studies and Promotion of Human Rights (Centro de Estudios Fronterizos y de Promoción de los Derechos Humanos, CEFPRODHAC) and the CNDH. To provide this context, and demonstrate that the patterns of abuse extend through multiple years, this chapter reviews nine torture cases documented by the CNDH in Tamaulipas between 1990 and 1996.

Juan Lorenzo Rodríguez Osuna

On November 28, 1996, State Judicial Police (Policía Judicial del Estado, PJE) arrested Juan Lorenzo Rodríguez Osuna in Tampico. Two days later, a state prosecutor accused him of committing a gruesome double murder that had allegedly taken place on November 13, 1996. Federal prosecutors also eventually charged him with drug trafficking. The irregularities—involving police, prosecutors, and the judge—began early and continued throughout the case. Despite this, Rodríguez Osuna was sentenced on state charges to twenty-five years in prison for murder and, in federal court, to ten years for drug trafficking. At this writing, the state murder charge has been appealed to a federal court, and the drug conviction has been overturned on appeal.

In a report filed on the day of the arrest, police said they set out in search of Rodríguez Osuna after hearing another man, Carlos Gutiérrez Zubieta, confess to

---

[111] Human Rights Watch interview, José Herrera Bustamante, Reynosa, Tamaulipas, November 21, 1997.

being Rodríguez Osuna's accomplice in the double murder.[112] According to the report, police, in the company of the witness, pulled over Rodríguez Osuna, who was driving in his truck. After the detainee allegedly insulted them, the officers took him to the station. The report continues: "Once at the station and after calming down, Juan Lorenzo Rodríguez Osuna, in the presence of Carlos Gutiérrez Zubieta, admitted having killed" the homicide victims.[113] According to Rodríguez Osuna, events unfolded differently. Police detained him, he maintains, then tortured and interrogated him for several hours, holding a gun to his head and repeatedly making him get in and out of the vehicle in which they held him.

Police taped an interrogation of Rodríguez Osuna that they said took place on November 28, 1996. On the tape, after the detainee repeatedly denies having committed the murder, he finally confesses. Attorney General José Herrera Bustamante told Human Rights Watch that Rodríguez Osuna's attorney was present during the interrogation,[114] which is denied by the detainee. Even though the tape was made by police, who are not permitted to take admissible statements from detainees, the judge accepted it as evidence.

The CNDH strongly criticized the state prosecutor in the case for consenting "to the arbitrary detention carried out by the judicial police."[115] The commission went on to criticize the fact that the prosecutor did not document the time or place of detention, nor when the police brought him to the police station—details that are fundamentally important for establishing the exact time at which the detainee came into police custody and, therefore, whether or not police had time to coerce him prior to handing him over to prosecutors. Authorities assigned a law student who had finished his course work but not received his degree as Rodríguez Osuna's public defender until his family assigned a private attorney, leading the CNDH to conclude that the defense until the private attorney took over had been "inadequate."[116]

Gutiérrez Zubieta was initially charged with aiding Rodríguez Osuna, but the judge eventually changed the accusation to "covering up" the murder, arguing that

---

[112] State Judicial Police of Tamaulipas, police report submitted by Alberto Balmori Garza, Juan José Camarillo Garza, José Carlo Enríquez Noyola, and Eusebio Rodríguez Matamoros, November 28, 1996.

[113] Ibid.

[114] Human Rights Watch interview, José Herrera Bustamante, Reynosa, Tamaulipas, November 21, 1997.

[115] National Human Rights Commission, Recommendation 117/97, in *Gaceta* 89 (Mexico City: Comisión Nacional de Derechos Humanos, December 1997), p. 61.

[116] Ibid., p. 63.

he had failed to report Rodríguez Osuna's acts earlier. Gutiérrez Zubieta told the prosecutor on November 28 that Rodríguez Osuna alone shot the two victims, then borrowed a knife and carved them up, threatening Gutiérrez Zubieta that he would be killed if he fled or reported the incident. Then, in the early morning of November 30, 1996, police say that Gutiérrez Zubieta awoke and demanded to amplify his statement. According to the official version of events, Gutiérrez Zubieta, who told the prosecutor he had forgotten two important points, requested that a particular public defender represent him as he amplified his statement; a police officer was dispatched to wake and bring the public defender to the prosecutor's office. This took place even though Gutiérrez Zubieta had a private attorney.

Gutiérrez Zubieta's amplified statement says that Rodríguez Osuna made him return to the scene of the crime the next day. There, Gutiérrez Zubieta claimed, Rodríguez Osuna made sure his victims were dead, mutilated them beyond recognition, and covered the bodies with branches. The declarant also added that after the murder, as the two returned to town in separate cars, Rodríguez Osuna signaled with his headlights to have him pull over. During that time, the amplified declaration states, Rodríguez Osuna carried three large bundles from the vehicle he was driving to the side of the road, although Gutiérrez Zubieta did not know what was in the bundles.[117] Police allegedly went to the spot where Gutiérrez Zubieta said the bundles had been dropped and found that they contained marijuana. It is this amplified statement that served as the only basis for the federal drug charge against Rodríguez Osuna. The statement also served to provide the state appeals judge who confirmed the murder sentence, Félix Fernando García Oitegón, with the only explanation of motive for the murder.[118]

Less than twenty-four hours after allegedly amplifying his statement on November 30, 1996, Gutiérrez Zubieta refused before a state judge to reconfirm it. Before a federal prosecutor on December 3, he again denied amplifying the statement. The case file that summarizes the proceedings from the point of view of the prosecutor's office notes that Gutiérrez Zubieta "did not want to sign, and Commander Yáñez told him that he was going to kill his family. [Gutiérrez

---

[117] Amplification of declaration made by Carlos Alfonso Gutiérrez Zubieta, November 30, 1996.

[118] According to the judge, "The motive that moved him to commit the crime was the fact that he wanted to take possession of the shipment of drugs that the deceased (José Gerardo Eraña) carried hidden in a double bed of his vehicle." Supreme Court of Justice of the State of Tamaulipas, sentence in criminal case 377/97, March 19, 1998, p. 38. Translation by Human Rights Watch.

Zubieta] commented that he wasn't going to sign if he didn't have his lawyer, so a guy who looked like a lawyer was called, but the declarant said that he was not his lawyer and that he did not know who that person was."[119] According to the prosecutor's summary, he finally signed the document under pressure. The statement was used in the murder case against Rodríguez Osuna.

Like the prosecutor, the state judge hearing the murder case was unconcerned about the serious allegations made by Rodríguez Osuna about his arrest and treatment and by Gutiérrez Zubieta's retraction of the amplified statement. In fact, the judge, Laura Andrea Gallegos Núñez, went out of her way to exclude evidence that favored Rodríguez Osuna. The autopsy of the two alleged murder victims suggests that Rodríguez Osuna could not have murdered the victims in the way described and that the bodies had been moved to the spot where they had been found. It also gives reason to believe that the bodies may not belong to the two people identified as the murder victims. She rejected these findings by saying the autopsy lacked credibility, but she did cite the autopsy when information could be used against Rodríguez Osuna. The bodies were quickly cremated, so no further examination of the victims could take place.

In reviewing the case file, Human Rights Watch also found three documents supposedly issued by the judge that were, in fact, issued on the prosecutor's stationery. Further, the judge showed a clear lack of concern for the procedural problems that had taken place in the case during the detention and prosecutor's investigations. She argued, for instance, that the tape of the interrogation submitted as evidence many months after the detention should be accepted as evidence because Rodríguez Osuna had recognized that it was his voice on the tape and that "the declarant did not question in any way the motive for his making the statement as he did." She contradicted herself shortly thereafter, however, when she noted that he "illogically [affirmed] that he had been threatened, with a pistol to his head, but from the content of the tape, it is not evident that any such threat existed."[120] The judge also accepted Gutiérrez Zubieta's amplification without questioning why he refused to ratify it.

The federal judge who heard the drug case, José Elías Gallegos Benítez, appears to have used all possible room for discretion in condemning Rodríguez Osuna to ten years' imprisonment. There was no physical evidence linking the accused man to the marijuana; only Gutiérrez Zubieta's retracted statement linked

---

[119] Ministerial Declaration made by Carlos Alfonso Gutiérrez Z., December 3, 1996.

[120] State Criminal Court of the Seventeenth Judicial District, sentence in criminal case 363/96, September 30, 1996, p. 23. Translation by Human Rights Watch.

Rodríguez Osuna to the drugs. As he did in state court, Gutiérrez Zubieta denied making the statement again in federal court. In a May 27, 1997 federal proceeding in which Gutiérrez Zubieta and Rodríguez Osuna faced each other, the following exchange took place:

Rodríguez Osuna: "Why are you blaming me for this crime?"

Gutiérrez Zubieta: "I was threatened into signing the declaration."

Rodríguez Osuna: "Who threatened you into signing the declaration against me?"

Gutiérrez Zubieta: "Commander Yáñez was the one who threatened me, putting a pistol to me. When I declined to sign it, he threatened my family. For those reasons I acceded to signing the declaration." [121]

The judge, however, cited the principle of procedural immediacy to accept the retracted amplified statement made by Gutiérrez Zubieta, arguing that supporting evidence existed.[122] In fact, of the seven pieces of "corroborating" fact, two were restatements of the charges and the rest were mere conjecture, such as the fact that the prosecutor had indeed found the marijuana and that the truck in which it was allegedly transported by Rodríguez Osuna was found to have a double bed.[123] With respect to the retraction, the judge argued, "It cannot be taken into consideration and is ineffective for stripping the validity from the first declaration [the amplification], given that there is insufficient evidence to support the veracity of his word, and, given the principle of procedural immediacy, the first statement made by the declarant should prevail."[124] The judge also cited precedent on "ineffective retractions" that itself cited the principle of procedural immediacy.[125]

Even though the judge cited other evidence that he said allowed him to favor the amplification of the declaration over the retraction, doing so also conveniently allowed him to avoid examining alleged human rights violations. Indeed, rather than question the way in which Gutiérrez Zubieta gave his alleged amplification, the judge found, "What Carlos Alfonso Gutiérrez Zubieta said turns out to be

---

[121] Transcript of court session, May 27, 1997.
[122] Tenth Federal Judicial District in Tamaulipas, sentence in criminal case 1/97, November 13, 1997, pp. 69-71.
[123] Ibid., p. 70.
[124] Ibid., p. 71. Translation by Human Rights Watch.
[125] Ibid., p. 72.

inexact, with respect to the fact that he was not assisted by his lawyers . . . ."[126] Rather, the judge argued, he had been aided by the law student who testified that Gutiérrez Zubieta had solicited his services. The case file makes no reference to any investigation of the circumstances under which the amplification was made.

Initially sentenced to ten years for possession of marijuana, the conviction was thrown out on appeal, essentially because Gutiérrez Zubieta's alleged amplified declaration did not indicate that he actually saw Rodríguez Osuna with the marijuana.[127] The appellate judge did not raise questions about any of the procedural problems encountered in the process. The Office of the Federal Attorney General informed Human Rights Watch that the federal prosecutor who indicted Rodríguez Osuna on drug charges had been punished for doing so, although the office did not specify the type of punishment he received.[128] It is encouraging that, on appeal, the federal drug conviction was thrown out. Nonetheless, the prosecutor and trial-level judge accepted evidence that strongly suggested that it had been fabricated and the declarant tortured, and the judge cited legal precedent to avoid showing concern. Given that such problems are part of a pattern, not an anomaly, authorities cannot justify tolerating poor judicial processes on the grounds that the appeals process may correct them. The responsibility of the government to ensure that human rights standards are met during criminal investigations starts when the detainee enters custody and continues throughout the process.

José Alfredo Ponce Reyes

Believing José Alfredo Ponce Reyes to be the man responsible for stealing a six-pack of beer from a Reynosa city convenience store, public security police approached him as he sat in his truck on September 5, 1997. When Ponce Reyes tried to flee, the police opened fire and gravely wounded the man, who was brain-damaged in the incident. According to police, Ponce Reyes's vehicle struck an officer, and they fired their weapons in the air in an attempt to get him to stop. Evidence exists to suggest that the police opened fire needlessly and recklessly, including testimony from an eyewitness who has said that no police officer was hit by Ponce Reyes's truck. After the shooting, police abandoned the victim and fled

---

[126] Ibid. Translation by Human Rights Watch.

[127] First Unified Federal Court of the Nineteenth District in Tamaulipas, sentence in criminal matter 185/97-1-B, June 19, 1998, pp. 86-87.

[128] Human Rights Watch interview, Eduardo López Figueroa, director, Internal Affairs, Office of the Federal Attorney General, Mexico City, June 12, 1998.

the scene, later giving contradictory statements to investigators about the way in which they fired their weapons.

Regardless of the circumstances of the shooting, the government failed to respond correctly to the incident. A proper investigation would probably have clarified any doubts about whether police acted appropriately or recklessly and should have led to their punishment, at a minimum, for having abandoned the victim. The investigation was marred by problems. For instance, the prosecutor failed to take testimony from the only eyewitness before concluding his investigation and submitting the case to a judge; the testimony was taken after the case was filed.

Police said they were searching for a man in a similar truck who had just stolen a six-pack of beer from a nearby Seven Eleven. They found no beer in the truck and did not encounter the knife used by the assailant. Ponce Reyes's truck had Wisconsin license plates, from the United States, similar in appearance to the Texas plates the Seven Eleven clerk had noted were on the get-away vehicle. The officers initially told investigating judicial police officers that they shot at the truck's tires.[129] In later statements, however, four of the five municipal police officers told prosecutors that they only fired warning shots into the air.[130] When the prosecutor indicted the officers, he made reference to the police report that said the officers shot at the truck's tires, but he never sought to clarify the contradiction. The fifth officer—from the passenger seat of the police car that blocked Ponce Reyes in front—claimed that his Uzi fired accidentally when he was knocked to the ground by a fleeing Ponce Reyes.[131] "I had the Uzi in my hand, and since the chamber was full, it fired," officer José Eduardo Ramírez González, who was in the passenger seat, told the prosecutor. "I didn't fire my weapon at that person or his vehicle."

An eyewitness explained to Human Rights Watch that Ramírez González's version of events was not correct, asserting that the officer had not left his patrol car and that he had not been struck by Ponce Reyes's vehicle. "Only one [police officer] got out of the car," the witness said. "The copilot absolutely did not get out of the car," the witness said, "and José did not hit anyone when he took off."[132]

---

[129] Police report filed by the Delta Group, September 5, 1997.

[130] Statement by the accused Juan Eduardo Garza Betancourth, September 5, 1997; statement by the accused Efrén Federico Alonso Méndez, September 5, 1997; statement by the accused Marcial Donato Díaz, September 5, 1997; and statement by the accused Rito Martínez Zúñiga, September 5, 1997.

[131] Statement by the accused José Eduardo Ramírez González, September 5, 1997.

[132] Human Rights Watch interview, witness, Reynosa, November 21, 1997.

The prosecutor indicted the five officers the day after the incident, charging them with "abuse of authority" and "causing wounds."[133] Despite the fact that state judicial police investigations immediately turned up the name of the same eyewitness interviewed by Human Rights Watch,[134] the prosecutor did not take her statement until more than a month after the incident—long after he formulated his charges.[135] Although the case file indicates that the prosecutor had asked police to notify the witness that her statement was wanted, the witness only gave her statement after a sister of the wounded man sought out the prosecutor in mid-October.[136] This witness's testimony would have had direct bearing on the version of events given by police. Her testimony directly contradicted the officers' statements that one of them had been hit by Ponce Reyes's car. Similarly, officials failed to take testimony from other witnesses to the aftermath, such as family members. "Not once did the police or prosecutor take my statement," the victim's mother told Human Rights Watch.[137]

The physical evidence seemed to contradict the police officers' statements; Human Rights Watch examined Ponce Reyes's truck, for instance, finding what looked like eleven holes made by what appeared to be bullets of three different calibers. Although Human Rights Watch could not determine with precision the details of the bullet holes, the Human Rights Commission of Tamaulipas State noted in a report on the case that the bullet holes came from more than one weapon.[138]

On September 8, a judge ruled that the police should be released on bail, since the crimes they were accused of committing were "not serious" according to the state penal code, even though the victim's life was in danger. The following day, the judge decided to move forward with the prosecutor's charge of causing wounds but ruled that there were no grounds that the officers had abused their authority. He argued: "There is no indication that the indicated preventive [police] agents went

---

[133] File 892/97, document 1951, September 6, 1997.

[134] Police report, September 5, 1997.

[135] Human Rights Watch interview, witness, Reynosa, November 21, 1997.

[136] Ibid.

[137] Human Rights Watch interview, María Elena Reyes de Ponce, Reynosa, November 21, 1997.

[138] Tamaulipas State Human Rights Commission, Recommendation 34/98, April 6, 1998, p. 20. The commission wrote that "the bullets found in José Alfredo Ponce Reyes's truck were fired by the weapons in possession of the Preventive Police agents."

overboard in the exercise of their functions."[139] The judge accepted the argument that the Uzi accidentally fired when an officer was knocked to the ground and that the other officers shot only into the air. The officers were released on bail that was, according to the victim's father, paid by the municipal government.[140]

When he indicted the officers, the state-level prosecutor noted that a federal crime may also have been committed by some of them. Two of the weapons used by the officers—a .45 automatic and the Uzi—appeared to be for the "exclusive use of the army," as established by the Federal Law of Firearms and Explosives.[141] He resolved to bring his finding to the attention of the federal prosecutors,[142] then turned over a certified copy of the file to his federal counterpart. The federal prosecutor never filed weapons charges, according to the Center for Border Studies and Promotion of Human Rights.[143]

In this case, police used excessive force to stop a fleeing suspect. As the United Nations Basic Principles on the Use of Force and Firearms by Law Enforcement Officials maintains, police officers shall not use their firearms unless they do so against the imminent threat of death or serious injury. Even if Ponce Reyes had initially posed a threat to one of the police officers, firing at the fleeing suspect after he had passed the officer would have been excessive. The police officers then abandoned Ponce Reyes when they thought he was dead. Their version of events—that they shot into the air or, in one case, fired accidentally—does not coincide with that of an eyewitness or with their initial statement to investigating police. In addition, the witness contradicts the police version indicating that the Uzi fired after the officer holding it was knocked to the ground by Ponce Reyes's truck. Further, the variety of bullet holes in the truck indicates that at least two separate weapons were fired at the vehicle, which makes it impossible for the accidental firing theory to be correct.

A prosecutor took testimony from a key eyewitness long after the case was submitted to the judge and never took statements from family members who were

---

[139] Second State Criminal Court of the Sixth District of Tamaulipas, resolution of judicial situation, criminal case 314/997, September 9, 1997.

[140] Letter from Heriberto Ponce to Dante Schiaffini Barranco of the National Human Rights Commission, May 27, 1998.

[141] Article 11(d) of this law holds, "Arms, munitions and materials for the exclusive use of the army, navy and air force are the following: automatic pistols, carbines and rifles, submachine guns, and [machine guns] of all calibres." Translation by Human Rights Watch.

[142] Office of the State Attorney General of Tamaulipas, indictment, September 6, 1997.

[143] Human Rights Watch telephone interview, Arturo Solís, president, Center for Border Studies and the Promotion of Human Rights, July 8, 1998.

on the scene shortly after the incident. Though he did have indications that the police had given two versions of their targets upon firing, he never followed up on this key contradiction. When he indicted the officers, he did so for minor charges, failing, for instance, to charge them with attempted murder. His failure to make even a mild case for "abuse of authority" led a judge to throw out the charge.

To his credit, the prosecutor did turn the file over to the federal prosecutors to investigate the possible arms law violation, but federal prosecutors never followed up on the issue.

Erick Cárdenas Esqueda

Municipal police in Nuevo Laredo detained Erick Cárdenas Esqueda, a teenager, on January 4, 1997, allegedly for participating in a street fight. Two hours later, he was found dead in his cell. Police maintain that he hanged himself, but physical evidence suggests he was tortured and then murdered. Authorities have failed to investigate the incident properly.

When discovered in the jail cell, Cárdenas Esqueda's body rested as if sitting on a cement bench, head tilted forward. A shirt, tied around his neck, extended to the bars of the window above. Police asserted that the bruises on Cárdenas's face resulted from the street fight that allegedly motivated his arrest. Cárdenas's body, however, also showed wounds that would have been impossible to receive in a fight but would have been consistent with torture: according to the state medical examiner's report, Cárdenas's testicles had been skinned.[144] Family members and witnesses said that the victim showed no bruises prior to his detention. "On the night that it took place, he had a problem with some neighbors. He came home afterward, but I clearly saw that he had not been beaten in the face. There was no blood," Patricia Esqueda, Cárdenas's mother, related to Human Rights Watch.[145] This was because the fight was broken up by neighbors before it came to blows, she said. Her testimony was consistent with that of witnesses to the detention.[146]

Evidence of murder also exists. According to photographs of Cárdenas taken after he died and reviewed by Human Rights Watch, his back showed two vertical indentations as if he were pulled back with extreme force into the bars of his cell. The marks could not have come from when he allegedly hanged himself, because the bars on which the shirt was tied were above, not behind, him.

---

[144] Medical report, January 5, 1997.
[145] Human Rights Watch interview, Patricia Esqueda de Cárdenas, Nuevo Laredo, November 20, 1997.
[146] Center for Border Studies and Promotion of Human Rights, "Caso Erick," Acta No. 03-97, Enero 1997.

There have been several irregularities in the case. Police detained Cárdenas without a warrant. At the time of arrest, there was no disturbance, according to witnesses interviewed by the Center for Border Studies and the Promotion of Human Rights, so there could not have been an "in flagrante" excuse for picking him up. Further, if Cárdenas had been badly beaten prior to detention, and had skinned testicles, police should have taken him to a hospital or provided medical attention at the station, which they did not do. Not until nine hours after the alleged suicide did authorities notify Cárdenas's mother. Almost a year later, investigators had still not taken official testimony from the mother, even though she saw her son just before his arrest and subsequent death.[147]

The National Human Rights Commission in Tamaulipas

The CNDH has issued at least ten recommendations involving torture in Tamaulipas from as early as the commission began to function in 1990. As explained above, Human Rights Watch reviews these cases here in order demonstrate that the abuses they feature are neither new nor isolated. Indeed, a review of CNDH torture cases from Tamaulipas, in the years 1990 to 1996, clearly shows how the system constructed to protect human rights and investigate and punish violations breaks down consistently at the three fundamental stages: police, prosecutors, and courts.

Police and torture

The most egregious abuses in the state occur at the police level in a predictable pattern. Almost without fail, in cases in which Federal Judicial Police were involved, the detainees were illegally held and tortured prior to being turned over to prosecutors. Common to almost every case is prosecutors' lack of initiative to follow up on torture allegations or medical exams that describe torture. In some cases, prosecutors simply fail to investigate torture, or they charge police with lesser crimes, such as "abuse of authority." In other instances, even if the human rights violator is indicted, authorities do not follow up on arrest warrants.

Each of these problems was clearly displayed in the case of Moisés Córdoba Sánchez, a sixteen-year-old who was tortured to death in a Tamaulipas prison on May 13, 1994. Prison guards bound, gagged, and stripped him, then forced him to dance naked. His tormentors raped him with a nightstick, then beat him with broom handles, apparently killing him. Afterward, in an informal punishment room, they applied electrical current to his body to make it appear he had been electrocuted.

---

[147] Human Rights Watch interview, Patricia Esqueda de Cárdenas.

Prison officials alleged that the inmate had committed suicide by biting exposed wires in the punishment room, a finding supported by a deficient medical exam by the doctor who initially examined the body. However, an examination of the body conducted by the CNDH, after an exhumation, showed that it would have been difficult for the inmate to have killed himself by biting the wire.[148] Rather, the CNDH concluded, the evidence led to the "well-founded presumption" that the victim was dead when brought to the punishment room and that the guards tried to make his death look like a suicide. Prison authorities were indicted for abuse of authority, battery, and making false statements, but not for torture or murder.[149] According to the Center for Border Studies and Promotion of Human Rights, the responsible parties remained free as late as August 1997.[150]

Torture also takes place after arbitrary or prolonged detentions, when authorities detain a suspect without a warrant or other valid justification or when they hold a detainee in excess of legally allowable limits. In the CNDH cases analyzed here, police detentions ranging from four days to a week were standard practice. On November 19, 1990, for instance, Federal Judicial Police officers detained Martín Arroyo Luna and José Brito Navarro for possession of illegal arms and other alleged crimes.[151] The detention itself did not violate the law, since the detainees were caught in flagrante. However, police proceeded to hold them far beyond the allowed time before turning them over to prosecutors, and tortured them in the meantime. Three days after their arrest, the victims confessed before the regional PJF commander under duress.[152] The case file contains multiple records of medical exams confirming that they had been tortured.[153] According to the CNDH, eleven officials were eventually fired, but none appeared to have been prosecuted.[154]

---

[148] National Human Rights Commission, Recommendation 24/95, in *Gaceta* 55 (Mexico City: Comisión Nacional de Derechos Humanos, February 1995), p. 177.

[149] National Human Rights Commission, *Informe anual de actividades mayo 1994-mayo 1995* (Mexico City: Comisión Nacional de Derechos Humanos, 1995), p. 115.

[150] Center for Border Studies and Promotion of Human, *Casos presentados al relator de la ONU en su visita a México*, August 1997, p. 9. Human Rights Watch did not obtain more recent data on the whereabouts of the perpetrators.

[151] National Human Rights Commission, Recommendation 73/91, August 23, 1991 (original version), p. 2

[152] Ibid., p. 4

[153] Ibid.

[154] National Human Rights Commission, *Tercer informe semestral junio-diciembre de 1991* (Mexico City: Comisión Nacional de Derechos Humanos, 1991), p. 81. In this report, the commission noted that the recommendation had been completely fulfilled. The officers

On June 12, 1996, when inmates at the Reynosa Social Rehabilitation Center escaped, prison guards captured and tortured two men, Armando Santos Orozco and Walter Ricardo Kavieses Soto. They appear to have executed a third man, Cecilio Hernández Herrera, whose death they tried to make seem like a suicide. According to testimony of one of the escaped prisoners, Hernández Herrera had shot and wounded a prison guard while escaping.[155] The CNDH found that prison officials' assertion that the man had killed himself was not probable, given that the bullet that killed him entered from the left side of his head but the gun was found near his right hand.[156] The CNDH also decried the prosecutor's failure to investigate the case properly.[157] None of the cases had been properly investigated by the time the CNDH issued its latest annual report, and no action appeared to have been taken with respect to the prosecutor who performed negligently in the false suicide incident.[158]

Medical exams

In several cases, the CNDH condemns medical reports in Tamaulipas as blatantly contradictory and incomplete. Lucas Mota Gallegos, Angel Rodríguez Aldaba, Rodrigo García Nino, and Ernesto Gallegos Hernández were arrested by the PJF on January 12, 1991, for drug possession and detained for two days during which time they signed confessions.[159] Medical reports about the detainees' condition contained "obvious contradictions."[160] In one exam, the doctors concluded that there appeared to be "no recent external injuries on any of the detainees." Another doctor, however, had reported just three days earlier that Lucas Mota Gallegos had a two-day-old head wound. According to the CNDH, a further exam was "conclusive in indicating that the wounds [received during torture] were

---

who were fired were not included in the report's list of state agents who had been prosecuted. Subsequent commission reports simply list the recommendation as fulfilled, without updating the 1991 commission report with respect to this case.

[155] National Human Rights Commission, Recommendation 105/96, in *Gaceta* 76 (Mexico City: Comisión Nacional de Derechos Humanos, November 1996), p. 140.

[156] Ibid., p. 145.

[157] Ibid.

[158] National Human Rights Commission, *Informe anual de actividades mayo 1996-mayo 1997* (Mexico City: Comsión Nacional de Derechos Humanos, 1997), pp. 186-87.

[159] National Human Rights Commission, Recommendation 91/92, May 11, 1992 (original version), p. 82

[160] Ibid., p. 88

inflicted with the aim of causing physical damage."[161] Arrest warrants were issued against three of the officers, who were detained. The CNDH never published follow-up information indicating what happened to the officers accused of torture. The torture victims were found guilty of drug-related crimes and sentenced in January 1992. One of the victims was also sentenced on a weapons charge.[162]

Prosecutors' reluctance to use medical exams clearly stymies their progress on torture cases, as happened in the Arroyo Luna and Brito Navarro case, described above. Equally obstructive is the simple lack of medical documentation of torture. For instance, in Recommendation 4/94, the CNDH found that PJF agents had illegally detained and tortured Manuel Equihua Cervantes and Fidel Martínez Flores in Reynosa city in September 1989. Medical examiners failed to note the bruises that resulted, however, so the PGR decided not to press torture charges against the officers.[163] According to the CNDH, the PGR reported in August 1994 that no action would be taken against the officials implicated in torture because, "Even if the victim, Manuel Equihua Cervantes, had bruises at the moment he made his preparatory declaration before the judge who tried him, they were never documented by medical examiners."[164] Given the lack of documentation, the PGR asserted that it would not file charges against the officers believed responsible. The other abuses could not be investigated because of the statute of limitations.

Prosecutors and torture

Prosecutors have two important roles to play in ending torture. First, they must consistently question evidence that may have been received through torture. In order to do so, they must also guard against the commission of procedural irregularities such as arbitrary detentions, which often precede torture. Second, they must fully investigate and prosecute allegations of torture, ensuring that lesser charges are not substituted for torture. In the Córdoba case, described above, in which prison guards raped and killed a sixteen-year-old boy, the prosecutor failed to charge prison officials with torture or homicide, for instance. The same can be seen in other CNDH cases, such as the detention and torture of Martín Moreno Espinoza in Reynosa on April 8, 1993. Moreno Espinoza slipped into a coma and died in August 1993, but despite medical reports showing that he had been tortured,

---

[161] Ibid., p. 89

[162] Ibid., p. 88.

[163] National Human Rights Commission, Recommendation 4/94, *Gaceta* 45 (Mexico City: Comsión Nacional de Derechos Humanos, April 1994), p. 48.

[164] National Human Rights Commission, *Informe anual de actividades mayo 1994-mayo 1995*, p. 447.

Torture and Extrajudicial Execution in Tamaulipas State   77

and witness testimony corroborating the torture, the prosecutor merely opened a "battery" investigation into the municipal Preventive Police who had detained him.[165] However, the officers were not even indicted on the lesser charge.[166] After the CNDH issued its recommendation, fourteen municipal Preventive Police in Reynosa were indicted for torture. The prosecutor was eventually suspended for fifteen days without pay for unduly dragging his feet in the investigation.[167] In addition, three of the officers were punished administratively with thirty-day suspensions without pay.[168] However, a judge never accepted the evidence of torture, so arrest warrants were never issued.[169]

Additional cases documented by the CNDH

In addition to the CNDH cases from Tamaulipas documented above, the commission has investigated the following torture cases in the state since 1990:

- In Recommendation 1/92, the CNDH found that PJF officers held Salvador Valero Saucedo, Santos Valero Saucedo, Reynaldo Estrada Montes, Perfecto Mireles Guzmán, and Juan Piña Ochoa in Reynosa for four days longer than permitted by law before turning them over to prosecutors. Arrested on April 25, 1990, they were accused of drug-related crimes. During the detention, they were repeatedly beaten and forced to sign confessions, and they were indicted.[170] The CNDH did not provide follow-up information on the beatings but did report—without elaboration—that the recommendation that the officers be investigated for the prolonged detention had been completely fulfilled.[171] As described above, the fact that the recommendation was

---

[165] National Human Rights Commission, 137/95, in *Gaceta* 64 (Comisión Nacional de Derechos Humanos, November 1995), pp. 233-35.

[166] National Human Rights Commission, *Informe anual de actividades mayo 1995-mayo 1996* (Mexico City: Comisión Nacional de Derechos Humanos, 1996), p. 106.

[167] National Human Rights Commission, *Informe anual de actividades mayo 1996-mayo 1997*, p. 542.

[168] National Human Rights Commission, *Informe anual de actividades mayo 1995-mayo 1996*, p. 108.

[169] National Human Rights Commission, *Informe anual de actividades mayo 1996-mayo 1997*, p. 542.

[170] National Human Rights Commission, Recommendation 1/92, in *Gaceta* 19 (Mexico City: Comisión Nacional de Derechos Humanos, February 1992), pp. 23- 24.

[171] National Human Rights Commission, *Informe anual de actividades mayo 1992-mayo 1993* (Mexico City: Comisión Nacional de Derechos Humanos, 1993), p. 193.

considered "completely fulfilled" does not necessarily mean that the perpetrators were ever brought to justice.

- In November 1991, the commission issued Recommendation 105/91, regarding the incommunicado detention and torture of Eloy Izazaga Acosta by Federal Judicial Police agents. Izazaga was forced to sign a false declaration admitting to transporting drugs. In fact, the doctor who practiced a medical exam on the detainee when he entered prison found that there was a well-founded possibility that he had been tortured.[172] Federal prosecutors eventually requested four arrest warrants for officials believed responsible. Of those requests, two were denied by the court and one was thrown out because of a procedural error committed by the prosecutor.[173] As of 1994, the most recent information on the case provided by the CNDH, the remaining warrant had been issued but not served.[174]

- In March 1994, the CNDH issued Recommendation 40/94, which found that PJF agents had illegally detained Trinidad Díaz García in July 1989, entering his home without a warrant and arresting and torturing him. The prosecutor held the victim in detention for too long before turning him over to a judge, failed to investigate the PJF abuses, and did not take judicial note of the victim's bruises. The medical examiner similarly failed to take note of the signs of torture.[175] The PGR decided to take no action against the officials, arguing that the statute of limitations prohibited them from doing so.[176]

---

[172] National Human Rights Commission, Recommendation 105/91, November 4, 1991 (original version).

[173] National Human Rights Commission, *Informe anual de actividades mayo 1992-mayo 1993*, p. 183.

[174] National Human Rights Commission, *Informe anual de actividades mayo 1993-mayo 1994* (Mexico City: Comisión Nacional de Derechos Humanos, 1994), p. 514.

[175] National Human Rights Commission, Recommendation 40/94, in *Gaceta* 45 (Mexico City: Comisión Nacional de Derechos Humanos, April 1994), p. 369.

[176] National Human Rights Commission, *Informe anual de actividades mayo 1996-mayo 1997*, p. 312.

VI. TORTURE AND EXTRAJUDICIAL EXECUTION IN OAXACA STATE

Located in the south of Mexico, Oaxaca is one of the country's poorest and most topographically and ethnically diverse states. Together with Guerrero, it is one of two states where EPR guerrillas have been most active and where authorities have reacted most harshly to suspected members of the group. The Loxicha region of Oaxaca became the focal point for the government's search for EPR members after Fidel Martínez, a former treasurer of San Agustín Loxicha, was killed in an EPR attack on a naval base on August 28, 1996. On that same day, the EPR attacked several targets throughout Mexico.

Unlike the EZLN in Chiapas, the EPR has conducted periodic armed attacks against government targets since its first armed appearance. In response, the government appears to have developed a strategy designed to obtain information from sources at all costs, while weakening the political or peasant-based organizations that authorities believe are linked to the guerrilla movement. In the cases documented below, torture and false confessions were used to implicate people as members of the guerrilla group. For the most part, neither prosecutors nor judges expressed concern about the abusive manner in which suspects came into custody or the torture suffered by detainees. In fact, the proceedures used by prosecutors ranged ranged from the highly questionable to the deeply disturbing. In several torture cases documented by the Mexico City-based Christian Action to Abolish Torture (Acción de los Cristianos para Abolir la Tortura, ACAT), prosecutors took no action on their own to investigate, despite medical records showing that the detainees had been tortured.

On September 25, soldiers and state and federal police carried out raids leading to the arrest of eleven people from San Agustín Loxicha, including the mayor and much of the town council. Over the following months, joint police-military operations netted further detainees. According to a group of Mexican NGOs and a defense lawyer handling Oaxaca cases, officials arbitrarily detained 127 people—torturing one hundred of them—and carried out thirty-two illegal searches and five executions.[177] In researching this report, our fieldwork focused on four representative torture and false-prosecution cases and an extrajudicial

---

[177] Acción de los Cristianos para la Abolición de la Tortura, Brigadas pro-Derechos Humanos Observadores por la Paz, Centro de Derechos Humanos "Fr. Francisco de Vitoria," Liga Mexicana por la Defensa de los Derechos Humanos, Unión de Pueblos contra la Represión en la Región Loxicha, Abogado Defensor Israel Ochoa Lara, and Comisión Mexicana de Defensa y Promoción de los Derechos Humanos, "Informe sobre hechos de tortura y otros tratos crueles, inhumanos o degradantes ocurridos en la región de Los Loxicha y otros lugares del Estado de Oaxaca," August 1997.

execution. The picture that emerges is one of uncontrolled abuse of force in the name of fighting the EPR, combined with a lack of concern on the part of officials throughout the justice system.

The abuses documented in the context of anti-EPR counterinsurgency are not the only human rights abuses that take place in Oaxaca. For this reason, we supplement our fieldwork with eight torture cases handled by the CNDH between 1990 and 1996, concluding that the problems identified in the EPR-related cases investigated by Human Rights Watch are neither new nor unique.

The Loxicha Region: Abuses in the Search for EPR Suspects
Illegal detention, forced confession, and torture

One of several sweeps through the Loxichas region occurred on November 7, 1996, three months after coordinated EPR attacks took place in several Mexican states. Nineteen people were arrested. Illegal arrests were followed by torture and prosecution. After his eventual release, one of the victims, Amadeo Valencia Juárez, explained to Human Rights Watch the circumstances of his detention and the torture to which he was subjected:

> At 5:00 a.m. on November 7 I heard footsteps outside, then banging on my door. Men dressed in black uniforms broke in and starting asking, "where are your guns." Then they searched the house. They took me to the municipal government building, where they made me kneel on the ground with my hands behind my head; the army was there, along with state and federal judicial police. At around 6:00 a.m., they took nine of us to the San Martín Ranch. They threatened to kill me, but left me and several others on the truck while they beat the ones they took off the truck. At around 5:00 p.m. they took all of us to Crucesita, where they kept us in a small, dark room for two days without giving us any food or water. We used bags and empty bottles if we had to go to the bathroom.
>
> They kept asking me to incriminate other people as members of the EPR and to sign blank sheets of paper. I refused. It was there that they started to beat me. They stripped me and attached electrodes to my testicles. "You're a member of the armed group," they said. "I'll let you go if you accuse your *compañeros*." On November 8, they tortured me again, promising to let me go if I signed blank sheets of paper, but this time they threatened to kill my family if I didn't. So, I signed the blank

pages. But they didn't let me go. I spent nine months in Ixtotel prison in Oaxaca, then five months in Almoloya in Mexico state.[178]

Similarly, Gerardo Ramírez Hernández told Human Rights Watch that his captors repeatedly ordered him to accuse other detainees, then forced him to sign blank sheets of paper.[179]

Questionable or illegally obtained statements were then used by proscutors in building their case. For instance, court documents confirm that a prosecutor used the statements of three detainees who accused another man of direct EPR participation, even though the detainees's declarations were made in Spanish, a language they do not speak; none of the three had a translator.[180] Prosecutors also used hearsay testimony against Prisciliano Enríquez Luna: one of the detainees testified that he had been told that Enríquez Luna was a member of the EPR; based on that evidence and his own forced declaration, Enríquez Luna spent a year in jail.[181]

The prosecutor in these cases alleged that the detainees had been arrested while at his office. He said he had issued the arrest warrants himself, without going to a judge, according to a lawyer for several of the detainees.[182] Using "urgency" provisions in the criminal code, the prosecutor argued—contradictorily—that the suspects had voluntarily gone to the prosecutors' office but that they would flee if he did not arrest them then and there. Without wasting time considering the detainees' mutually reinforcing allegations of the mass arrest and subsequent torture, the judge accepted the prosecutor's story. The judge did so despite evidence that the prosecutor had falsely accused at least some of the detainees, bringing into question the prosecutor's actions in the case. In other cases, the judge accepted retracted confessions on the grounds that the detainees had failed to prove that they were retracting their statements because of physical and psychological threats.[183]

After winning an appeal, six of the November 7, 1996, detainees were released a year later, a positive development given the procedures used against

---

[178] Human Rights Watch interview, Amadeo Valencia Juárez, January 28, 1998, Oaxaca, Oaxaca.

[179] Human Rights Watch interview, Gerardo Ramírez Hernández, January 28, 1998, Oaxaca, Oaxaca.

[180] Sentence in criminal case 316/97-II, December 5, 1997, p. 111.

[181] Ibid., p. 113.

[182] Human Rights Watch interview, Israel Ochoa, January 28, 1998, Oaxaca, Oaxaca.

[183] Ibid., p. 104.

them. The judge threw out statements falsely attributed to the men who did not speak Spanish, because they did not have a translator.[184] He made no comment, however, regarding what kind of procedure could have been used to obtain such declarations. The cases raises serious concern about how the prosecutions could have moved forward in the first place, and why accusations of torture were not investigated. Roberto Antonio Juárez, Priciliano Enríquez Luna, and Virgilio Cruz Luna were released without charge, but their accusations of torture—supported by medical documentation—were not investigated until they were released. Only after ACAT took up the cases did prosecutors begin to investigate, but ACAT was required to conduct much of the research that would permit the investigation to move forward. Given that authorities did not move on the case while the victims were in detention, the prosecutor rightly argued that, after their release, it was much harder to locate them for investigation-related interviews.

Extrajudicial execution

On April 24, 1997, Celerino Jiménez Almaraz died in Santa María Jalatengo, San Mateo Río Hondo municipality. According to his wife, he was arbitrarily detained and executed. According to police, the man ambushed police officers and died after being wounded in an armed confrontation. In our investigation, we found compelling evidence that the man was, in fact, executed by police. At this writing, authorities have done little to clarify the incident.

María Estela García Ramírez, who was married to the victim, explained to Human Rights Watch how police entered her home on the night of April 24, shooting into the air and then following her husband as he tried to flee.

> They didn't ask for anyone in particular. My husband tried to run, but they shot him in the left foot. He made it out the door, but I didn't know how much farther he got. Later, we followed the trail of small drops of blood to a place where there was a lot of blood and regurgitated food.[185]

Police gave a completely different story to investigators. According to a report filed by two state judicial police group leaders, sixteen state judicial police agents gathered at midnight in Santa María Jalatengo to begin a hike to Juquilita, San Agustín Loxicha, in order to serve two arrest warrants. The police divided into

---

[184] Ibid., p. 111.

[185] Human Rights Watch interview, María Estela García Ramírez, Mexico City, September 3, 1997.

two groups, one of which included five officers. According to testimony from the police, about ninety minutes into the strenuous hike, the first group was ambushed, and the five officers responded by throwing themselves to the ground, returning the fire, and calling for support from the second group. The assailants moved from about twenty meters to four or five meters from the police before the shooting ended. When it did, the police said, they found an injured Jiménez Almaraz. According to several police statements, officers "immediately" carried him back to the trucks at Jalatengo.[186]

On June 6, one of the group leaders who initially reported on the attack filed an additional report, adding a detail that had not been mentioned by any of the officers who had given testimonies after the incident. According to officer Hugo T. Chávez Cervantes, when police discovered the injured man, they asked his name and where he lived, and were told that he lived in Los Limares. "So we proceeded to interview people who live in the community, to see if they knew a Celerino Jiménez Almaraz, which they strongly denied." Chávez continued that only after conducting these interviews did they proceed back to the trucks at Jalatengo.[187] According to the police, Jiménez Almaraz died while being transported back to town.

The physical evidence was consistent with an execution, not a death in a shoot-out in the dark. According to the medical examiner, the body had seven seven-millimeter holes formed in a circle with a twenty-centimeter radius in the front left side of the thorax. The left forearm bore five seven-millimeter bullet wounds. The trajectory of the bullets was from up to down.[188] This finding suggests that Jiménez Almaraz was shot at close range by someone with the time to aim carefully, not at all the circumstances described by the police in their reports. Further evidence that the man was executed came from the prosecutor himself, who examined the body and reported that the wounds on the thorax showed a "gunpowder tattoo" and that those of the forearm were "impregnated with gunpowder."[189] Gunpowder markings such as these could only result from close-range firing, not the four or five meters that police say was the closest they got to the alleged assailants when they were exchanging gunfire. Also inconsistent with the suggestion of a shoot-out was the prosecutor's inability to find bullet

---

[186] The police version of events is taken from internal police documents filed by officers after the incident and by statements made to prosecutors.

[187] Hugo T. Chávez Cervantes, report filed with the director of the State Judicial Police, June 6, 1997.

[188] Autopsy report on Celerino Jiménez Almaraz, April 24, 1997.

[189] Prosecutor's report on transport of cadaver, April 24, 1997.

casings when he examined the site of the alleged confrontation the following day.[190]

On the evening following the incident, the prosecutor began a murder investigation. However, the same judicial police officers involved in the confrontation, from Pochutla, were assigned to carry out the investigation, in an obvious conflict of interest. The Fray Francisco de Vitoria Center for Human Rights (Centro de Derechos Humanos "Fray Francisco de Vitoria"), which had been handling the case on behalf of the victim's wife, asked state prosecutors to transfer responsibility for the investigation from Pochutla to the state attorney general's central office in Oaxaca city. At the same time, the center provided an address in Oaxaca to receive all notifications of official, case-related actions, such as requests the prosecutors might make to interview witnesses.[191]

In November 1997, the attorney general's office shifted responsibility for the case to Oaxaca investigators but notified the center neither of the change in oversight nor of February 1998 summonses for Jiménez Almaraz's family members to testify, even though the center legally represented the family. Similarly, authorities did not notify the center of a summons for Jiménez Almaraz's widow, which had been left with her family members in rural Oaxaca, an area to which the widow, fearing for her safety, had not returned since shortly after the attack that killed her husband. By failing to utilize the Oaxaca city address, prosecutors effectively ensured that the human rights group would not be able to assist the victim's family members and make sure they were not coerced during their testimonies, and it guaranteed that the victim's widow would not learn of the summons for her to testify. It was not until September 1998, when a center staff person based in Mexico City visited the family, that the center learned of the summonses and brought the widow to testify.[192] A request made by the center in September 1998 to obtain a copy of the case file was rejected by the prosecutor, thereby making the center's examination of the prosecutor's actions difficult and impeding the center from submitting case documents to intergovernmental or international human rights organizations.

---

[190] Prosecutor's report on physical inspection of the scene, April 24, 1997.

[191] The center is based in Mexico City and does not maintain an office in Oaxaca. It provided the address of a Oaxacan human rights group to receive official notifications.

[192] Human Rights Watch interview, Adriana Carmona, Centro de Derechos Humanos "Fray Francisco de Vitoria," Washington, DC, December 6, 1998.

The National Human Rights Commission in Oaxaca

Consistent with the pattern found in CNDH cases from other states, torture in cases in Oaxaca often followed arbitrary arrest and incommunicado detention. In many Oaxaca torture cases, medical examiners failed to document abuses or prosecutors failed to initiate torture investigations, or both. The victims, however, were consistently prosecuted for crimes they may or may not have committed, while judges rarely paid attention to the procedural irregularities or torture documented during the process.

As of June 1998, based on the most recent CNDH information available, no torturer has been sentenced based on CNDH recommendations related to Oaxaca. In three cases, federal prosecutors decided not to press charges, sometimes based on questionable reasoning suggesting that the victim had been pressured into changing his story. For instance, Federal Judicial Police agents arbitrarily detained Donato Geminiano Martínez on August 17, 1993, torturing him in order to force him to confess to a drug-related crime.[193] The federal prosecutor failed to investigate the torture, despite the evident wounds.[194] The first medical exam carried out on August 17, when Martínez was first picked up, showed no signs of physical mistreatment; an exam after the incommunicado detention showed signs of torture.[195] After the CNDH issued its recommendation in May 1995, the PGR began an investigation, but reported that Martínez retracted his earlier allegation that he had been tortured, saying instead that he had received his wounds in a motorcycle accident the day before his arrest.[196] However, the motorcycle incident would not have explained why medical exams documented bruises only after he had been in detention, nor why the initial prosecutor had failed to investigate the allegations of torture.

Torture prosecutions were not even successful in cases in which medical documentation showed signs of torture. State judicial police detained Otilio López Aragón and Armando López Pimentel on October 20, 1992, holding them illegally for two days and torturing them to induce self-incriminating statements.[197] Medical

---

[193] National Human Rights Commission, Recommendation 57/95, in *Gaceta* 58 (Mexico City: Comisión Nacional de Derechos Humanos, May 1995), pp. 47 and 52.

[194] Ibid., p. 52.

[195] Ibid.

[196] National Human Rights Commission, *Informe anual mayo 1996-mayo 1997*, pp. 493-94.

[197] National Human Rights Commission, Recommendation 172/93, in *Gaceta* 39 (Mexico City: Comisión Nacional de Derechos Humanos, October 1993), pp. 105 and 110-11.

exams confirmed the torture. In its 1996 annual report, the CNDH reported that three officers had been charged with "abuse of authority," not torture, but no arrest warrant had been executed.[198] On May 10, 1996, the officers voluntarily turned themselves in, but they were released with a warning.[199]

In one of the only CNDH Oaxaca cases in which authorities were punished in relation to torture, the victim was so badly injured that he later died of his wounds. On December 3, 1995, Federal Judicial Police in Salina Cruz detained Rafael Toledo Nolasco, whom they accused of having drugs and a weapon reserved for the exclusive use of the armed forces.[200] They beat him so severely during the detention and later at the attorney general's office that he died a month later. Before he died, however, he was turned over to a federal prosecutor, charged, and transferred to a detention center. Prosecutors never questioned why he was in such a precarious physical condition, and decided not to press charges against the officers.[201] After the CNDH issued Recommendation 106/96 on November 6, 1996, detailing the problems in the case, the Office of the Federal Attorney General suspended for thirty days the prosecutor who failed to investigate Toledo Nolasco's physical condition. They fired the prosecutors who decided not to press charges against the police, ordering that they be barred from working for the institution for ten years. The two police officers were fired and eventually charged with torture and murder. A judge issued arrest warrants for the men, but the former officers fled and remain at large.[202]

Additional Cases Documented by the CNDH

- Federal Judicial Police detained and tortured Rufino José Jiménez on October 7, 1991, forcing him under torture to sign a self-incriminating statement, according to the CNDH. He was indicted, prosecuted, and sentenced for possession and sale of marijuana, possession of marijuana seeds, and

---

[198] National Human Rights Commission, *Informe anual mayo 1995-mayo 1996*, p. 354.

[199] National Human Rights Commission, *Informe anual mayo 1996-mayo 1997*, p. 403.

[200] National Human Rights Commission, Recommendation 106/96, in *Gaceta* 76 (Mexico City: Comisión Nacional de Derechos Humanos, November 1996).

[201] Ibid.

[202] Office of the Federal Attorney General, "Resultados obtenidos por la Procuraduría General de la República en materia de lucha contra la impunidad y de los trabajos de la CNDH," document prepared for Human Rights Watch, June 1998.

possession of a weapon reserved for the use of the army.[203] The prosecutor never investigated Jiménez's allegation that he was tortured. The PGR decided not to press charges against the police, citing an assertion by the victim's defense lawyer to the effect that his defendant was not tortured during interrogation and that Jiménez had told him that his wounds had been caused during a struggle over a weapon with one of the arresting agents.[204]

- On August 28, 1993, municipal authorities in San Miguel Huautepec, and the son of one of them, tortured sixteen-year-old Tomás José Gómez Guerrero, tying his hands and feet, hitting him, and subjecting him to mock execution.[205] The men accused the youth of having hit a municipal police officer. Two days later, he was turned over to a nearby state prosecutor, who failed to document the physical evidence of the beating Gómez Guerrero had suffered, even though a medical examiner had already certified the wounds.[206] Gómez Guerrero was prosecuted for allegedly having hit the police officer. Arrest warrants were eventually issued against two of the authorities, for abuse of authority and illegal detention, but an appeals judge ruled that the warrants should not be executed.[207]

---

[203] National Human Rights Commission, Recommendation 8/94, in *Gaceta* 45 (Mexico City: Comisión Nacional de Derechos Humanos, April 1994), pp. 74-75.

[204] National Human Rights Commission, *Informe anual mayo 1995-mayo 1996*, pp. 401-02.

[205] National Human Rights Commission, Recommendation 39/94, in *Gaceta* 45 (Mexico City: Comisión Nacional de Derechos Humanos, April 1994), p. 360.

[206] Ibid., p. 367.

[207] National Human Rights Commission, *Informe anual mayo 1994-mayo 1995*, p. 469-70.

VII. "DISAPPEARANCES" AND THE JUSTICE SYSTEM

The very nature of "disappearances"—whereby authorities secretly detain and hold victims incommunicado, often torturing them to extract information—makes solution of such cases through the justice system extremely difficult. Such case require urgent reaction from authorities, since they are often followed by murder. Appealing to authorities to utilize the police and court systems often seems a hopeless cause, since by definition the detention has not officially been acknowledged and is usually being deliberately kept secret. Authorities committed to the protection of human rights insist on searching for the victims until they are located. Officials who are not equally committed may perform perfunctory searches, at best. In the cases reviewed in this chapter, police and prosecutors took the latter approach. In some cases, half-hearted searches where undertaken, while in others as much as a year went by before family members of the victims were even called to provide information. In several "disappearance" cases documented below, victims were transferred from unacknowledged military detention to the official custody of prosecutors, who failed to acknowledge any wrongdoing on the part of military officials involved. In others, the whereabouts of the victims remain unknown.

In the 1970s, as many as 400 real or alleged leftist guerrillas "disappeared" as part of a dirty war undertaken by the military in Mexico. These abuses conformed to a pattern practiced by military governments throughout Latin America during that time period, and took place in the context of Mexican guerrilla movements in several states. Current "disappearances" in Mexico fall into three main types. The first, reminiscent of the 1970s, consists of "disappearances" related to the conflict between government forces and the EPR. In some instances, these "disappearances" are temporary and followed by acknowledged detention and prosecution. In other cases, the victims' whereabouts remain unknown. Such cases are not examined in this study.[208]

Another type of "disappearance" takes place in the context of drug trafficking and counternarcotics efforts. The Mexican military has taken on a fundamental role in the battle against drug traffickers in Mexico. The Alejandro Hodoyán and Fausto

---

[208] For further information on "disappearances" carried out in the context of counterinsurgency operations, *see* Inter-American Commission on Human Rights, "Report on the Human Rights Situation in Mexico," para 145; Centro de Derechos Humanos "Fray Francisco de Vitoria" and Comisión Mexicana para la Defensa y Promoción de los Derechos Humanos, "Informe sobre desapariciones forzadas en México," October 1997; Centro de Derechos Humanos "Miguel Agustín Pro Juárez," "Desapariciones forzadas o involuntarias: 1986-1988," 1998; and Amnesty International, "Mexico 'Disappearances:' a Black Hole in the Protection of Human Rights," May 7, 1998.

Soto Miller cases, documented below, are examples of drug-related temporary "disappearances" carried out by the military. These cases may have taken place in a context in which one Mexican drug cartel was using active-duty army personnel in a battle for supremacy over another. But even if the motivation of the officers who commanded the operations involving Hodoyán and Soto Miller were private, the abuses were committed by state agents, and civilian prosecutors were ready to accept both detainees when the army was through with them without asking any questions.

The Inter-American Court of Human Rights has annunciated standards for official responsibility for "disappearances" carried out by authorities acting in a private capacity. "Any exercise of public power that violates the rights recognized by the Convention is illegal," the court noted, continuing,

> This conclusion is independent of whether the organ or official has contravened provisions of internal law or overstepped the limits of his authority: under international law a State is responsible for the acts of its agents undertaken in their official capacity and for their omissions, even when those agents act outside the sphere of their authority or violate internal law.[209]

The clandestine incarceration of Hodoyán and Soto Miller was illegal and should have been the subject of investigation and prosecution. In the case of Hodoyán, a U.S. citizen, a U.S. law-enforcement agent interviewed him several weeks into his detention, and although he knew that Hodoyán was being illegally held and reported this to the U.S. Embassy, no action was taken to assist the man. In fact, closing their eyes to the manner in which Hodoyán was detained, U.S. officials arranged to further debrief the victim in the United States, where he was eventually sent; when he later fled the United States, he was "disappeared" again, and remains missing as of this writing. A witness to the second "disappearance" identified a member of a federal counternarcotics police unit as having carrired out the second "disappearance." In the Soto Miller case, the victim was sentenced to forty years in prison for a crime he was said to have committed when, all indications are, he was actually in unacknowledged military detention.

Finally, "disappearances" have also been carried out by police-led gangs involved in drugs and kidnappings, as in the case of José Alberto Guadarrama,

---

[209] Inter-American Court of Human Rights, Velázquez Rodríguez judgement of 1988, para. 170.

from Morelos state, documented below. Guadarrama, a former state judicial police officer, was apparently detained by other officers. Police were able to commit this abuse by virtue of the authority vested in them by the government and were encouraged to do so by the consistent failure of the state to investigate or punish such crimes. The Guadarrama case, it turns out, was symptomatic of a broader problem in Morelos state, where the highest-ranking police officials were eventually jailed after police were caught dumping the body of a kidnap victim in neighboring Guerrero state.

Alejandro Hodoyán

On September 11, 1996, soldiers detained Alejandro Hodoyán, a U.S. citizen by birth, in Guadalajara, Jalisco state. They believed him to be a member of the Arrellano Félix drug cartel. Although Hodoyán was held in secret detention by the military, police may also have been involved. After pumping him for information on the Arrellano Félix operation for several months, soldiers turned him over to federal prosecutors. Both military and civilian officials hoped that he would testify against other alleged members of the Arrellano Félix drug cartel, including his own brother. Hodoyán was eventually given immunity from prosecution in Mexico if he would do so.[210] U.S. officials were also interested in debriefing Hodoyán. Alerted that a potentially valuable source of information was in military custody, an agent of the Bureau of Alcohol, Tobacco, and Firearms (ATF) interviewed Hodoyán several weeks into his secret detention. Later claiming incompetence on the part of a key embassy official, U.S. consular authorities did nothing to help Hodoyán. More interested in the source's information than in protecting human rights, U.S. law-enforcement authorities also did nothing to aid the man, thereby becoming complicit in the violations he suffered. In fact, without being bothered by the way Hodoyán had come to be detained, or the treatment he received, they arranged for him to be sent to the United States to serve as a witness in drug cases.

In order to get the victim to cooperate, the army subjected him to successive rounds of torture. According to an unsigned statement he later gave to his family, soldiers tortured him intermittently for weeks. He recalled that on the day of his detention,

> They put a pillow case over my head, with me lying down on a bed, one person on top of my upper body and another on my legs. My arms were

---

[210] Julia Preston, "Mexican Tale: Drugs, Crime, Torture and the U.S.," *New York Times*, August 18, 1997.

handcuffed to the head of the bed and my feet to the other part, where the feet go. They started to throw water on my face, which was covered by the pillow case. I started to suffocate. That's when the questions started.[211]

The questions on his first day of detention had to do with people he had recently met whom the soldiers believed were involved with drug trafficking. Faced with answers they found unacceptable, the soldiers threw him in a car, drove him around, then returned to what Hodoyán believed to be the same location. This time, they wrapped him in a blanket with his head and feet protruding from the ends. Again they threw water on his covered head, and applied electric current to the soles of his feet and eyelids. They questioned him more about people and phone numbers he had with him when detained. After two more days of torture, then some sleep, Hodoyán was questioned on September 14 about the assassination of federal prosecutor Ernesto Ibarra Santés, stationed in Baja California, who had been gunned down that same day in Mexico City. Hodoyán was also questioned about a July 22, 1996 shootout between soldiers and drug traffickers in Guadalajara in which two soldiers had died. The Arrellano Félix brothers had attempted to kill rival drug trafficker Amado Carrillo, killing the soldiers instead.[212]

When Hodoyán failed to arrive in Tijuana as expected on September 11, his family began to search for him, seeking help from both Mexican and U.S. officials. His family heard nothing from him until the following month. According to the *New York Times*, which covered the Hodoyán story as part of a Pulitzer Prize-winning series on drug trafficking in Mexico, soldiers broke Hodoyán in a matter of days, turning him into a consummate source of information. In reference to the army general who headed the government's counternarcotics agency at the time, the newspaper reported, "In late October General Gutiérrez Rebollo was sufficiently confident of his new informant's cooperation that he allowed him to call his family and tell them he was still alive."[213] After the first phone call, his family told Human Rights Watch, they installed a caller identification apparatus on

---

[211] Unsigned statement by Alejandro Hodoyan, March 3 and 4, 1997. The statement was made after Hodoyán's release from military custody and before he again "disappeared." After the second "disappearance," the document was signed by the family members to whom he recounted the events.

[212] Preston, "Mexican Tale."

[213] Ibid.

the telephone; when he called again, they noted the number from which he had called, then called back. The line was answered, "Fifth [military] region."[214]

A U.S. State Department official familiar with the case told Human Rights Watch that several weeks after his "disappearance," a U.S. law enforcement agent—identified in the *New York Times* as belonging to the ATF—interviewed Hodoyán. "In the course of the interview and after considerable time, he learned that the guy might have had a claim to U.S. citizenship," the official told Human Rights Watch. Implying that the agent knew that Hodoyán was in illegal detention, he continued, "When he realized that, the agent knew he [the agent] didn't want to be there. He told the appropriate U.S. embassy officials about the guy, and the officials all relied on the appropriate authority, the consul general, to do something about it."[215] Apparently, the consul general never did.

The Office of the Federal Attorney General did not respond to Human Rights Watch's request for information about the Hodoyán case, but even if Hodoyán's own statements are not taken into account, it is clear that he was held illegally by the military. In court documents from an unrelated case involving military corruption, soldiers admitted to holding Hodoyán. Sgt. Vicente Ruiz Martínez testified on March 8, 1997, for instance, that he had guarded Hodoyán in Guadalajara and also during a trip made by the detainee to Mexico City on September 14, 1996; another soldier testified that he participated in the detention in September of a man whose nickname was "Alex," which is what Hodoyán's family called him.[216] If the detention had been legal, he would have been held in civilian, not military custody, even if soldiers participated in the original arrest.

The encounter with the U.S. agent led to interest from U.S. law-enforcement agencies in a more thorough debriefing of the captive, but not, apparently, in providing a remedy for the egregious human rights violation he was suffering during his clandestine detention. In mid-December, Hodoyán signed papers allowing U.S. officials to take him to San Diego, a trip that finally took place in February 1997. On February 20, disheartened by the questioning aimed at incriminating his brother, Hodoyán left the hotel in which he was located and returned to his family in Tijuana in a psychologically troubled state.[217]

---

[214] Human Rights Watch interview, family members of Alejandro Hodoyán, Baja California, May 4, 1998.

[215] Human Rights Watch interview, Washington, D.C., September 4, 1998.

[216] Ministerial declaration of Vicente Ruiz Martínez, March 18, 1997 and declaration of Cabo de Trans. Ramón Caetano Polino Alcala, February 19, 1997.

[217] Human Rights Watch interview, members of Alejandro Hodoyán's family, Tijuana, Baja California, May 4, 1998.

On March 5, armed men pulled him from the passenger seat of a car that his mother, Cristina Palacios Roji Siliceo, was parking in Tijuana. She recalled,

> When I got into the parking spot, I turned to get some documents from the back. I saw a van pull up very quickly, and the first thing I saw was two men getting out with machine guns. "What's going on?" I asked my son. "Once again, the same guys," he responded. They grabbed him by the neck. I was yelling, "Who are you? What do you want? Where are you taking him?" The same guy who had put Alex in the van aimed at me—I was looking at him for two or three seconds, which is why I didn't forget his face. When they put him in the van, the doors were left open, so I ran and got in. "Leave him alone. Leave him alone," I yelled. My son told me, "Go away, Mom." The guy took my arms and threw me out.[218]

Palacios Roji Siliceo immediately went to prosecutors, having a clear image in her head of the man who had faced her with his weapon drawn. She had noted, too, the van's license plate number. The plate number was eventually traced back to a vehicle that had been impounded and was in the custody of Federal Highway Police. Investigators had Palacios Roji Siliceo speak to an official artist, who, based on her description, reproduced the face of the man she remembered. Eventually, she identified the man from a picture in a PGR employment file, and, as part of the investigation, identified him in person in September 1997.[219] According to a Mexican newspaper, the man was Ignacio Weber Rodríguez, the head of anti-drug intelligence at what was, at the time of Hodoyán's "disappearance," the National Institute for the Combat of Drugs, the PGR's counternarcotics agency.[220] The PGR did not respond to a Human Rights Watch request for information on the status of the case against the agent.

It is not at all clear what officials are doing to locate the victim, and as of mid-August 1998, the Hodoyán family had no information regarding the prosecution of the man identified by Hodoyán's mother as responsible for the abduction.[221]

---

[218] Human Rights Watch interview, Cristina Palacios Roji Siliceo, Tijuana, Baja California, May 4, 1998.

[219] Ibid.

[220] Anita Snow (Associated Press), "Anti-Drug Chief Weber Accused in Kidnap, Torture," *The News,* September 4, 1997.

[221] Human Rights Watch telephone interview, Cristina Palacios Roji Siliceo, August 13, 1998.

Human Rights Watch is aware of no punishment for authorities who participated in or tolerated the arbitrary detention, "disappearance," or torture that began in September 1996. Moreover, the case raises serious questions about the willingness of prosecutors to use blatantly illegal processes, including "disappearance," in the name of fighting drugs. The seamless transfer of Hodoyán from secret military detention to official custody, and then to the United States, demonstrates a troubling ends-justify-the-means approach to Mexican and U.S. counternarcotics efforts.

U.S. complicity in the initial "disappearance" of Hodoyán is deeply troubling. Even if the State Department's version of events is true—that the failure of consular officials to aid Hodoyán stemmed solely from the consul general's negligence[222]—U.S. law-enforcement officials moved forward with plans to further interview Hodoyán after the ATF agent learned that he was a U.S. citizen and in secret military custody.

Fausto Soto Miller

According to Fausto Soto Miller, soldiers detained him on September 12, 1996, tortured and interrogated him, held him in unacknowledged detention for sixteen days, then turned him over to civilian prosecutors. During this period, his family searched for him in vain. For their part, prosecutors announced that Soto Miller had been detained on September 27—not the 12th—while caught in the act of guarding a drug lord's safehouse. The Mexican press quoted a statement by the military labeling Soto Miller a leading drug trafficker.[223] According to his family, Soto Miller had nothing to do with drug trafficking but was picked up because Alejandro Hodoyán, who had been detained by the same soldiers the day before, had had his name with him.[224] Whether or not Soto Miller is linked to the drug cartel, all the evidence suggests that his version of temporary "disappearance" and prosecution on fabricated charges is correct.

In a letter from prison, Soto Miller recalled his treatment when detained on September 12. In addition to referring to his torturers by name, he described their acts:

---

[222] Human Rights Watch interview, State Department official, Washington, D.C., September 4, 1998.

[223] "Positiva, la intervención del Ejército contra el narcotráfico," *Excélsior* (Mexico City), August 12, 1997.

[224] Human Rights Watch interview, family members, Mexico City, June 6, 1998.

The first of them connected cables to my toes, and he turned on the power. Later, he beat my heels with a board. The second person interrogated me and threatened me. They also tortured me by placing rags over my face, asphyxiating me, and putting water up my nose and in my mouth to choke me, in those moments applying electrical current that got progressively stronger.[225]

Soldiers in Guadalajara held him for sixteen days before turning him over to civilian prosecutors. During the time he was in unacknowledged detention, soldiers' inquiries included questions about the July 22, 1996 confrontation between drug traffickers and soldiers in Guadalajara. They also flew him to Sinaloa state to identify houses belonging to drug traffickers.

Evidence from an unrelated court case corroborates Soto Miller's version of events. In the trial of Gen. Jesús Gutiérrez Rebollo, the former anti-drug chief jailed for his ties to traffickers, Sgt. Vicente Ruiz Martínez recalled how on September 12 and 13, 1996 he was in Guadalajara, where he helped to guard several detainees.[226] On September 14 he was sent to Mexico City, and he returned the next day; rather than remain in Guadalajara, though, the soldier was immediately ordered to travel to Culiacán, Sinaloa state. In his testimony about those events, he recalled that on the airplane, "they brought onto the plane one of those who had been at the Fourth Company and whom he knows goes by the name of Fausto Miller. . . ."[227]

Even though Soto Miller had been in detention since September 12, the federal prosecutor's office falsely announced in early October 1996 that they had arrested Soto Miller on September 27, alleging that he was a body guard of Tijuana drug cartel leader Ramón Arrellano Félix.[228] They filed drug trafficking and arms charges against him, asserting that he had been arrested in an Arrellano Félix safe house containing multiple high-caliber weapons and marijuana.[229] According to court documents, Federal Judicial Police said that the arrest was made when they coincidentally flew over the house in a helicopter and noticed two vehicles in a

---

[225] Fausto Soto Miller, letter from prison, October 10, 1997. Translation by Human Rights Watch.

[226] Ministerial declaration of Vicente Ruiz Martínez, March 18, 1997.

[227] Ibid.

[228] Juan Manuel Venegas, "Culpa Lozano a los hermanos Arellano Félix del asesinato de Ibarra Santés," *La Jornada*, October 3, 1996.

[229] First Federal District Court in the State of Mexico, sentence in criminal case 105/96, May 29, 1998.

partially covered garage that matched the description of the vehicles used in the July 22 confrontation with soldiers.[230] When they saw Soto Miller run from the house, according to the official police report, they called for backup, and the suspect was apprehended. When arrested, the officers reported, Soto Miller spoke about the illegal contents of the safe house and his own participation in the Arrellano Félix gang. These same topics formed the substance of the official statement he was alleged to have made to prosecutors on the day of his alleged arrest.[231]

According to Soto Miller, however, the soldiers who had illegally detained him on September 12 turned him over to federal prosecutors on September 27. The prosecutors forced him to sign a prepared statement that he was not allowed to read, which he signed "Fausto Lie" (Fausto Mentira), instead of Fausto Miller. According to his public defender, the detainee did not have a lawyer with him when forced to sign the statement.[232] Instead, as Mexican law permits, he had "people of confidence" there. According to the public defender, however, the "people of confidence" were actually employees of the attorney general's office; neither responded to summonses to explain what happened during the time the statement was signed.[233]

Soto Miller was tried and convicted on June 1, 1998, and sentenced to forty years in prison for possession of prohibited weapons, possession of drugs, and criminal association based on what was alleged to have happened on September 27. In sentencing the defendant, the judge, Humberto Venancio Piñeda, rejected Soto Miller's retraction of the statement he was forced to sign. Rather than requiring clarification of the procedures used in the case, the judge argued, "Regarding the affirmations made repeatedly by the accused that he was detained on September 12 ...there are no documents that sufficiently prove it such that the retraction should be given legal validity."[234] Army officers identified by Soto Miller as participating in the September 12 detention or subsequent torture denied such involvement in court, and the judge cited their denials in his sentence.[235] The judge refused to admit as evidence the court documents from the Rebollo case indicating that Soto

---

[230] Ibid.

[231] Ibid.

[232] Human Rights Watch telephone interview, Héctor Sergio Pérez Vargas, July 2, 1998.

[233] Ibid.

[234] First Federal District Court in the State of Mexico, sentence in criminal case 105/96, May 29, 1998, p. 67.

[235] Ibid., p. 70.

Miller had been in detention since September 12, in part because the statements were not made in his courtroom.[236] Overall, the judge showed greater interest in convicting the defendant than in ensuring that serious human rights violations had not taken place during the judicial process.

The judge did express concern about Soto Miller's story of detention and torture, ordering the prosecutor to investigate it. According to Soto Miller's defense lawyer, the prosecutor said he found no evidence of torture or illegal detention, although the investigation officially remains open.[237] Soto Miller's defense lawyer has appealed the conviction.

As in the Hodoyán case, the Soto Miller incident raises several profoundly troubling issues: soldiers carried out the "disappearance" in violation of international law, but the justice system appeared ready to overlook the problem in the name of fighting drug trafficking. The federal attorney general's office did not answer Human Rights Watch queries about this case.

"Disappearance" and the Failure of the Morelos State Justice System

On January 28, 1998, Federal Highway Patrol officers discovered the commander of the Morelos state Special Anti-Kidnapping Group and two state judicial police officers disposing of the tortured body of Jorge Nava Avilés.[238] The victim, who had been kidnapped the day before, reportedly died during a torture session. The Morelos law-enforcement officers tried to dump the body in Guerrero state, along the highway between Iguala and Cuernavaca. The case, which received widespread press attention, led to the downfall of many Morelos public officials, including the governor of the state, who resigned. After investigating the Nava Avilés case, the CNDH described the extent of the involvement of Morelos state officials in crime and cover-up:

> In the state of Morelos, some members of the justice system have generated a climate of public insecurity, a product of the wave of kidnappings, homicides, torture, abuse of authority, and other illegal acts, committed by or consented to by those members. This has caused

---

[236] Ibid., p. 68

[237] Human Rights Watch telephone interview, Héctor Sergio Pérez Vargas, July 2, 1998.

[238] The Morelos case preceded a similar problem in Chihuahua state, where the leaders of a federal unit responsible for investigating drug-related kidnappings were reportedly found to be responsible for some of the kidnappings they were supposed to be investigating. Associated Press, "Elite Mexican Police Recalled," May 21, 1998.

a climate of corruption and impunity that benefits the intellectual and material authors of these crimes. This situation has resulted in the justice system not carrying out its appropriate functions, such as investigating and prosecuting crimes.[239]

The federal government quickly took control of the case under anti-organized crime laws; the state attorney general and head of the state judicial police were charged with trying to covering up the Nava Avilés torture and murder.[240] While it is encouraging that federal authorities acted so quickly in the case, it is equally noteworthy that they had failed for years to pay attention to evidence that Morelos police agents were engaged in kidnappings, "disappearances," and torture. Press reports from Morelos often repeated accusations made by victims and their family members regarding the involvement of police officials in such illegal acts. Indeed, at the time of the Nava Avilés murder, federal authorities had been engaged in discussions about the "disappearance" in early 1997 of José Alberto Guadarrama from Morelos—and its concomitant exposé of the problems in Morelos—with the Inter-American Commission on Human Rights.

"For at least two years it has been clear that the justice system was rotten," says Morelos state congressman Juan Ignacio Suárez Huape.[241] "There were protests, but on the state level, the leaders were involved with the criminals. On the federal level, there was no response, given the influence of [ex-Governor] Jorge Carrillo Olea. Despite the evidence, the investigations went nowhere." In December 1997, Suárez Huape organized a roundtable discussion on "disappearances," torture, and impunity.[242] Only after the Nava Avilés killing however, did prosecutors use the documentation he had long collected to prosecute state officials.

Prior cases had long gone uninvestigated because the very state officials responsible for doing so were involved in many of the kidnappings. One such case

---

[239] National Human Rights Commission, Recommendation 25/98, in *Gaceta* 92 (Mexico City: Comisión Nacional de Derechos Humanos, March 1998), p. 142. Translation by Human Rights Watch.

[240] "Former Morelos judicial officials released on bail," *Universal Journal*, March 10, 1998; "Conceden libertad bajo caución a Pedro Merlo y Miyazawa," *La Jornada*, March 10, 1998.

[241] Human Rights Watch telephone interview, July 15, 1998.

[242] *See* "Desaparición forzada de personas, tortura e impunidad en Morelos," a report produced by the Morelos state Congress's Justice and Human Rights Commission, based on a roundtable discussion held on December 9, 1997.

involved José Alberto Guadarrama García, a former state judicial police officer in Morelos state, who was detained in Emiliano Zapata city on March 26, 1997, by members of the state judicial police anti-kidnapping squad.

Elvira García Avelar, Guadarrama's mother, was with him when he was arrested, and she identified one of the arresting officers as José Luis Beltrán Velázquez, from the anti-kidnapping squad. Responding to a complaint the next day, state prosecutors initiated a fruitless search for the victim. On March 29, according to ACAT and the Center for Justice and International Law (CEJIL), which filed a complaint about the "disappearance" before the Inter-American Commission on Human Rights, family members of the victim were told by a guard at a state attorney general's detention center that Guadarrama had been brought in on the 26th but that he was sent to a state prison. Family members did not find him at the state prison, and the same official at the detention center later denied that Guadarrama had been taken there.[243]

Authorities did open an investigation into the "disappearance," during which Beltrán Velázquez denied any responsibility for the incident.[244] On April 4, Guadarrama's mother filed a request for amparo, roughly similar to habeas corpus, naming Mexico City and Morelos state justice and police authorities as responsible for the detention.[245] On May 21, a judge denied the writ on the grounds that the authorities said to be responsible for the detention had denied the accusation and García Avelar had not proven that they were responsible.[246]

Authorities failed to move on the case until late October 1997, after ACAT and CEJIL filed their complaint with the Inter-American Commission. On October 28, an arrest warrant was issued for Beltrán Velázquez, who had long since resigned from the police force and gone into hiding.

As the Inter-American Court of Human Rights has ruled, federal governments cannot avoid responsibility for the actions of state-level authorities by claiming that their federal system of government shields them when federal agents are not involved in human rights violations. Official tolerance of human rights violations is itself a human rights violation. This principle clearly holds in the case of Mexico.

---

[243] Acción de los Cristianos para Abolir la Tortura and Center for Justice and International Law, document submitted to the Inter-American Commission on Human Rights, August 22, 1997.

[244] Comparecencia Previa Presentación de José Luis Velázquez, April 3, 1997.

[245] Request for amparo, April 2, 1997 (received April 4, 1997), Elvira García Avelar.

[246] Judgement of amparo 233/97, May 21, 1997, Cuernavaca, Morelos.

The Suspected "Disappearance" of Verber, Verber, and Beltrán

Rogelio Verber Campos, Raúl Verber Campos, and Cecilio Beltrán Cavada were last seen on January 6, 1997, in Baja California state. Two days later, the Verber family received a phone call from a man who refused to identify himself, indicating that the Verber Campos brothers had been detained by a group of people dressed in dark uniforms and driving a Suburban vehicle with polarized windows. A few hours later, they received another call, this time indicating that the brothers had been moved to a military base.[247] In this case, no direct evidence links government officials to the fate of the missing men. Human Rights Watch's fear that they may have been "disappeared" by state agents, however, has been strengthened by authorities' failure to investigate the case properly, despite repeated efforts by the families of those involved.

The Verber family had been under suspicion by the authorities for drug-related offenses. On September 12, 1996—one day after Alejandro Hodoyán "disappeared" and the same day that soldiers illegally detained Fausto Soto Miller—soldiers surrounded the family home in Tijuana. Federal attorneys, acting with a warrant, searched the premises for the Arellano Félix brothers, finding neither the brothers, nor drugs, nor guns.[248] Rogelio Verber, the father of the missing brothers, informed Human Rights Watch that, off and on after September 12 and prior to the "disappearance" of his sons, he had observed unmarked cars parked outside his house.[249]

On January 10, 1997, the families of the three men filed a request for amparo in state and federal courts, arguing that the men were being held by the military. In response, a federal judge ordered an end to the incommunicado detention.[250] On behalf of the judge, an agent of the court went to police offices and military bases in Tijuana on January 10. None admitted to holding the men; at the Tijuana military garrison, the agent was told to come back later by officials who refused to give their names.[251] The following day, the agent was told that the men were not there. Similar searches carried out after family members named additional possible places of detention were also fruitless.

---

[247] Human Rights Watch interview, Rogelio Verber, father of the missing brothers, Tijuana, Baja California, June 3, 1998.
[248] Office of the Federal Attorney General, National Institute for the Combat of Drugs, Acta Circunstanciada, September 12, 1996.
[249] Human Rights Watch interview, Rogelio Verber.
[250] Ruling on amparo, Judge Pablo Jesús Hernández Moreno, January 10, 1997.
[251] Report filed by court agent, January 1997.

On January 13, Raúl and Rogelio Verber's father sought help from the state police,[252] but state authorities never interviewed him about the complaint he had filed.[253] Eighteen months later, using the control number that prosecutors assigned to the case when the complaint was initially lodged, Human Rights Watch sought information regarding what action had been taken on behalf of the brothers. "No such file exist," was the official response.[254] On March 4, 1997, the Verber family and relatives of several other missing men filed a formal complaint with the PGR. Displaying an outrageous disregard for the urgency required, it was one year later to the day that federal authorities finally interviewed the Verber family about the complaint.[255]

Unlike the Hodoyán and Soto Miller cases, in the Verber and Beltrán case there is no hard evidence to link the "disappearance" of the three men to state agents. We know, however, that the Verber family had been under surveillance since soldiers moved against Hodoyán and Soto Miller. The failure of federal authorities to investigate the case promptly raises serious questions regarding the government's concern for finding the missing men.

---

[252] Office of the State Attorney General of Baja California, Volante de Canalización, January 13, 1997.

[253] Human Rights Watch interview, Rogelio Verber.

[254] Human Rights Watch telephone interview, Leonardo Cortez Téllez, director of investigations, Baja California state attorney general's office, June 3, 1998.

[255] Human Rights Watch interview, Rogelio Verber.

VIII. IMPUNITY AND PUNISHMENT FOR HUMAN RIGHTS VIOLATIONS IN MEXICO

"Impunity" may be the most common word employed by nongovernmental human rights organizations to describe the Mexican government's response to abuses. For its part, Human Rights Watch has scarcely issued a report on Mexico without examining the failure of the government to respond adequately to human rights violations. Indeed, the theme of impunity runs throughout this report. However, as pervasive as the state's negligence is, it would be incorrect to assert that no human rights violators are ever investigated, prosecuted, or brought to justice in Mexico. To understand how and why the system so routinely fails, therefore, we must also ascertain how, why, and to what extent the system sometimes works.

This chapter draws on five cases of torture, or torture combined with execution, that were submitted to Human Rights Watch by the PGR and four torture or execution cases submitted by Mexico's Foreign Ministry, all of them provided in response to numerous Human Rights Watch requests for cases that these entities felt had been properly handled by authorities. It also reviews two cases investigated by nongovernmental human rights organizations in which police officers guilty of torture or extrajudicial execution have been brought to justice, and certain torture cases handled by the Mexico City Human Rights Commission (Comisión de Derechos Humanos del Distrito Federal, CDHDF), a governmental agency. In addition, it draws on cases analyzed in prior chapters of this report.

On numerous occasions during 1997 and 1998, Human Rights Watch solicited information from the Foreign Ministry and PGR regarding human rights cases they believed had been dealt with properly by authorities.[256] Such information would permit Human Rights Watch to factor into its analysis the government's response to frequent criticisms of impunity. After all, precisely at the time that Human Rights Watch was beginning field work for this report, the Foreign Ministry was arguing that there was no impunity for torture in Mexico.[257]

---

[256] Human Rights Watch meeting, Armando Alfonzo, personal secretary to Attorney General Jorge Madrazo, September 1, 1997; letter to Armando Alfonzo, September 9, 1997; Human Rights Watch meeting, Attorney General Madrazo, January 26, 1998; letter to Attorney General Madrazo, February 14, 1998; Human Rights Watch meeting, Ambassador Aida González, technical secretary of the Foreign Ministry's Interministerial Commission for Attention to Mexico's International Human Rights Commitments, and María Amparo Canto, the commission's congressional liaison, January 20, 1998; letter to María Amparo Canto, February 8, 1998; letter to María Amparo Canto, March 13, 1998; and Human Rights Watch meeting, María Amparo Canto, June 5, 1998.

[257] Foreign Ministry, press release 142, May 9, 1997.

In response to the Human Rights Watch requests, the Foreign Ministry sent a package to Human Rights Watch in March 1998 that consisted only of a 1992 press release issued by the CNDH (regarding a case in which no action was taken against alleged torturers), a section on torture from the commission's 1997 annual report, the Mexican Constitution, state and federal laws, and United Nations materials. After receiving the information, Human Rights Watch again solicited case-specific detail. On August 28, 1998, we received a package containing eleven cases culled from CNDH materials. Eight of the eleven did not relate to torture or other violent abuses committed by state agents, so we do not review them here.[258] Of the three cases relevant to the Human Rights Watch request—regarding torture committed by police or soldiers—no official was actually in custody.

The PGR also prepared a report for Human Rights Watch that included statistics and information on five human rights cases.[259] Four out of five came to the attention of the attorney general's office through the CNDH, an indication of the commission's importance as well as a sign that the PGR should develop better procedures for encouraging direct complaints and learning of cases on its own; as effective as the CNDH is on some cases, it cannot substitute for rapid action on human rights cases by the authorities who are initially responsible for handling them. Human Rights Watch notes that in none of the cases was a torturer serving a sentence. In one case, the accused fled, and in two others judges had yet to issue the requested arrest warrants. However, in two of the cases, torturers and two accomplices were in jail awaiting trial. Of the five cases documented below, the Rodríguez Tapia torture-murder deserves particular attention, because the PGR learned of the abuse through the press, not the CNDH, and within months had succeeded in putting the police officer who had tortured and killed Rodríguez Tapia behind bars while the case is being investigated.

---

[258] One of the eight cases involved a murderer who had been wrongly released from prison. He was not a government employee, however.

[259] Office of the Federal Attorney General, "Resultados obtenidos por la Procuraduría General de la República en materia de lucha contra la impunidad y de los trabajos de la CNDH," document prepared for Human Rights Watch, June 1998. The five selected cases were not presented as the only successfully resolved cases but rather as examples of the types of success achieved by the Office of the Federal Attorney General. In discussing the office's report with Human Rights Watch, the office's director of internal affairs stressed that during 1997 more public servants were fired than fined, the opposite of 1996 and an indication of what he said was an improvement in the quality of sanctions imposed on office employees. He also pointed out that since December 1996, when Jorge Madrazo took over as attorney general, they had given 184 human rights courses to 8,682 people.

Shades of Justice

Two fundamental measures of success in human rights cases are whether the officials responsible for torture, "disappearance," or extrajudicial execution serve prison time, and whether the government compensates the victim. By these measures, Mexico's record is exceedingly poor. At its rhetorical best, the Foreign Ministry argues that only eight people have been successfully prosecuted for torture, but the ministry does not even assert that those torturers are actually serving their sentences. In its most recent annual report, the CNDH noted that between May 1997 and May 1998 a total of thirty-nine public servants were indicted for human rights crimes based on commission recommendations, an increase over the twenty-eight documented in its prior annual report but a marked decrease from the 161, ninety-six, and seventy in years past.[260] The commission, however, does not maintain statistics on the final outcome of the cases it documents, so no global figures regarding convictions are available.

Despite daunting obstacles, in rare cases prosecutors have obtained guilty sentences against torturers or authorities responsible for extrajudicial executions. In the Manríquez case, documented below, a Mexico City police officer who permitted a subordinate to torture was sentenced under the Federal Law to Prevent and Punish Torture, although he was released after paying a fine, rather than serving time in prison, and the accused torturer himself was freed on a technicality. The Garci Crespo case, also analyzed below, led to the sentencing of four Mexico City public security police officers for the victim's extrajudicial execution.

Short of serving prison time, human rights violators may be detained during prosecutorial investigation or prior to sentencing, although these measures do not ensure ultimate punishment. Three federal police agents in cases described to Human Rights Watch by the PGR were arrested and jailed pending the outcome of their trial. It is far more common, however, for human rights abusers to have arrest warrants pending against them, to be at liberty while the subject of a half-hearted investigation, or not to be investigated at all.

It is insufficient for representatives of the executive branch of government to argue that their responsibility lies only in investigating charges of torture and, if warranted, indicting suspects. First, prosecutors control the speed and seriousness of their investigations, both of which frequently limit the success of prosecutions.

---

[260] National Human Rights Commission, *Informe anual mayo 1997-mayo 1998*, p. 681; *Informe anual mayo 1996-mayo 1997*, p. 623; *Informe anual mayo 1995-mayo 1996*, p. 577; *Informe anual mayo 1994-mayo 1995*, p. 579; *Informe anual mayo 1993-mayo 1994*, p. 681.

Second, human rights violations and procedural errors—including the failure to adequately investigate allegations of torture or other irregularities—routinely go unpunished, meaning that public officials accept, and therefore encourage, such violations.

It is also insufficient for the Mexican government to be satisfied with partial steps toward justice in torture cases. Administrative actions against torturers or those who permit it may be taken in addition to criminal actions, but they cannot substitute for prosecution and punishment by time in prison. Similarly, the opening of a criminal investigation for torture is a positive step, but it does not satisfy international law requirements that torturers go to prison.

Overcoming Obstacles in Human Rights Cases

From the cases analyzed in this report, it is clear that time plays an important role in impunity in Mexico, because the justice system's slowness in prosecuting perpetrators allows them to flee, valuable evidence is lost, or family members and human rights groups pushing for justice are forced to give up. In the Guadarrama case, for example, the officer responsible for the "disappearance" was able to watch without fear as the judicial process went nowhere; despite detailed information indicating that he was responsible, authorities did not act against him until Mexican and international human rights groups took up the case. When authorities finally indicted the suspect seven months after the "disappearance," and long after sufficient evidence existed to move against him, the officer slipped away.

Given that so many torture victims in Mexico are themselves prosecuted, the passage of time also makes it more difficult to obtain valuable evidence in torture cases. If torture victims remain in jail or prison for extended periods of time, they may be subject to prolonged pressure to retract their complaints. Several cases in Oaxaca, documented above, appear to have followed this pattern. At the same time, if prosecutors delay in taking statements from torture victims while they are in jail, and thus easily accessible, they may find it difficult to do so if the victim is released, as happened in several EPR-related torture cases documented in the chapter on Oaxaca.

The results generated by Mexico City's official human rights commission also highlight an important aspect of Mexico's justice system: with the right pressure from the right government official, the system can be pushed to prosecute human rights violators. In one case followed by the commission, city prosecutors charged torturers with "abuse of authority," a charge for which bail is available. When the commission's president learned of the lesser charge, he urged prosecutors to amend the case to reflect that the victim had been tortured, and he eventually succeeded. By the time the charge had been changed, however, the suspects had fled.

The Sisyphian role of Mexican governmental and nongovernment human rights organizations in promoting justice for human rights violations is important to highlight. Human rights cases in Mexico usually follow a pattern: the authorities initially deny that any violation took place, even in the most blatant cases. This leaves human rights groups saddled with the responsibility of documenting the abuses the state ignores. Even then, when the authorities ignore even the most well-documented cases, human rights groups are burdened with creating public pressure in favor of prosecution.

The sheer number of abuses in Mexico, however, makes it impossible for human rights organizations to take action on all cases. First, prosecutors must be hounded to investigate. When proseucutors do not, human rights groups often find themselves gathering the information that would permit an indictment, locating witnesses, for instance, and bringing them to prosecutors. Second, organizations spend valuable time meeting with authorities to urge them to ensure that prosecutors act on the information they do have, or to request copies of case files that would allow them to evaluate progress. Third, working with the news media to stimulate public pressure on government officials is time-consuming, and human rights groups easily produce more information than journalists can cover.

Victims' relatives also often play an important role in moving cases forward. In the Garci Crespo case, a family member worked full time for almost two years to persuade reluctant authorities to indict the police officers responsible for the extrajudicial execution of Garci Crespo. Those officers are now in prison, serving sentences. In Tamaulipas state, the parents of Juan Lorenzo Rodríguez Osuna have worked nationally and internationally on behalf of their son, traveling to Mexico City, sending expensive packages of materials to human rights organizations, and hiring private lawyers.

The inescapable conclusion of this chapter is that if the victim or the victim's family has time, money, and education, it is more likely that a human rights violator will be punished or a wrongly prosecuted individual freed without charge. Years of fighting through the courts or the news media may be necessary to obtain even a partial victory, so only those willing and able to put in a long-haul fight can hope for such results. Hiring a private lawyer, being able to travel to Mexico City or other areas to promote the case, and understanding the local and foreign news media are the keys to having a realistic chance of success.

Cases Deemed Successful by the PGR
Torture and execution victim Rafael Toledo Nolasco

On December 3, 1995, Federal Judicial Police in Salina Cruz, Oaxaca, detained Rafael Toledo Nolasco, whom they accused of possession of illegal drugs and a weapon reserved for the exclusive use of the armed forces. They beat him so seriously during the detention and later at the attorney general's office that he died a month later. Before he died, however, he was turned over to a federal prosecutor, charged, and transferred to a detention center. Prosecutors never questioned why he was in such a delicate state of health, and decided not to press charges against the officers.[261] After the CNDH issued recommendation 106/96 on November 6, 1996, detailing the problems in the case, the PGR suspended for thirty days the prosecutor who failed to investigate Toledo Nolasco's physical condition. They fired the prosecutors who decided not to press charges against the police, ordering that they be barred from working at the institution for ten years. The two police officers were fired and eventually charged with torture and murder. A judge issued arrest warrants for the men, but the former officers fled and remain at large.[262]

Extrajudicial execution victim José Soto Medina

On October 21, 1994, Federal Judicial Police agents illegally entered the home of José Soto Soto and Rosaura Medina Barajas, on the El Limoncito ranch, Apatzingán municipality, Michoacán state. They detained Soto Soto and his son Wulfrano Soto Medina, but executed another son, José Soto Medina. The police planted a gun on the victim and asserted that he had repeatedly shot at them before being killed himself. A CNDH examination of the body, however, showed that the victim was killed by a gunshot from between 25 and 35 centimeters away and that, before being shot, he had been beaten with what appeared to be a rifle butt. Based on this evidence, the commission concluded that José Soto Medina had been executed. Although police asserted they entered the home to serve an arrest warrant, no warrant for arrest or search was ever found. In a process plagued by irregularities, the prosecutors simply accepted the police version of events and decided not to prosecute the officers involved in the death of Soto Medina. In contrast, Soto Soto and Soto Medina were charged with drug and weapons violations.[263]

A prosecutor who participated in the detention was eventually charged with "crimes against the administration of justice," but an arrest warrant issued against him had not, according to the PGR's information, been executed as of June 1998.

---

[261] National Human Rights Commission, Recommendation 106/96, in *Gaceta* 76 (Mexico City: Comisión Nacional de Derechos Humanos, November 1996).

[262] Office of the Federal Attorney General, "Resultados obtenidos."

[263] National Human Rights Commission, Recommendation 112/96, in *Gaceta* 76 (Mexico City: Comisión Nacional de Derechos Humanos, November 1996), pp. 239-40, 246, and 247.

The administrative investigation into one police official stalled but remains open, as the official absconded. Arrest warrants were solicited for seven other police officers, accused of "crimes against the administration of justice," carrying out an illegal search, and violation of individual guarantees, but as of this writing a judge had not issued the warrants.[264]

Torture victim Donaciano Tapia Villalobos

On August 21, 1995, Federal Judicial Police agents detained Donaciano Tapia Villalobos and his brother-in-law, Victorino Jiménez Bera, in La Peñita de Jaltemba, Nayarit state. They were accused of possession of opium paste. According to Tapia Villalobos, the federal police transported him to the police station in the bed of a pickup truck, turning the muffler to face toward the bottom of the truck bed, stripping off his shirt, forcing him face down on the bed of the truck, and beating him on the back. Police reported that the detainee was burned when he voluntarily laid face down on the truck bed for the duration of the journey to the police station. The prosecutor to whom police delivered Tapia Villalobos failed to document the burns and bruises suffered by the detainee, and the medical examiner at the PGR documented only the burns, not the bruises. The statement initially made by Tapia Villalobos to the prosecutor was forced and later disavowed by the victim.[265]

After receiving a CNDH recommendation on February 20, 1997, the PGR conducted an administrative investigation that resulted in the firing of the two police officers responsible for transporting Tapia Villalobos to the station. One was prohibited from working for the force for five years and the other barred for ten.[266] The prosecutor was fired, but the medical examiner faced no sanction. At the same time, one federal police officer was indicted on torture and abuse of authority charges and arrested on July 21, 1997. Two other officials were arrested for covering up the abuse.[267]

Torture victim Juan Antonio García Carrillo

Federal Judicial Police arbitrarily detained Juan Antonio García Carrillo on November 6, 1995, in Piedras Negras, Coahuila state, holding him incommunicado

---

[264] Office of the Federal Attorney General, "Resultados obtenidos."

[265] National Human Rights Commission, Recommendation 4/97, in *Gaceta* 79 (Mexico City: Comisión Nacional de Derechos Humanos, February 1996), pp. 61-64 and 71.

[266] Office of the Federal Attorney General, "Resultados obtenidos."

[267] Office of the Federal Attorney General, "Resultados obtenidos."

until November 8. They beat him and threatened to puncture his testicles with syringes if he did not give the police the information they wanted. When the detainee asked for an explanation, he was hit in the right eye, causing blurred vision.[268] The CNDH concluded that he was a victim of torture, since "there is proof that the wounds suffered by Juan Antonio García Carrillo in particular were maliciously produced by the arresting agents, not as a consequence of his detention, but with the intention to get him to confess to criminal acts he never committed."[269] The following day, police tried to force him to sign a false confession, providing him with a "person of confidence" who was not, in fact, of his own choosing. He, along with three other people, was accused of possession of heroin. Three of the four were indicted, but two of those, including García Carrillo, were eventually acquitted almost a year later. To his credit, the judge hearing the case refused to accept the testimony forcibly extracted from García Carrillo and the other detainees.[270]

Two police officers were indicted on abuse of authority charges, despite the fact that the CNDH had documented that torture had taken place. As of this writing, arrest warrants had not been issued; nor had the PGR finished administrative investigations into the officials who failed to act properly in the case: the prosecutor who charged the detainees based on fabricated evidence and failed to question the mistreatment they suffered; the detainees' public defender; and medical personnel who failed to document the physical evidence of abuse.[271]

Torture-murder victim Agustín Rodríguez Tapia

Federal Judicial Police acting without a warrant or other legal cause detained Agustín Rodríguez Tapia on August 9, 1997, and took him to the PGR office in Mexicali, Baja California state. They beat him during the detention and again at the PGR office. As a result of the beatings, Rodríguez Tapia died.

The PGR informed Human Rights Watch that within hours of learning of the abuse through a newspaper account, an investigator was sent to check into the story.[272] An investigation was opened on August 27, 1997, and three police officers were indicted a month later, one for murder, one for covering up the abuse, and all

---

[268] National Human Rights Commission, Recommendation 69/97, in *Gaceta* 84 (Mexico City: Comisión Nacional de Derechos Humanos, July 1997, p. 254.
[269] Ibid., p. 267. Translation by Human Rights Watch.
[270] Ibid., pp. 260 and 262.
[271] Office of the Federal Attorney General, "Resultados obtenidos."
[272] Human Rights Watch interview, Eduardo López Figueroa, director, internal affairs, Office of the Federal Attorney General, Mexico City, June 12, 1998.

three for abandoning a person in need.[273] On October 26, 1997, a judge issued an arrest warrant for the officer charged with murder and abandonment, who was subsequently jailed. The judge denied the request for arrest warrants against the other two officers. The PGR also has administrative investigations pending against all three officers.

Cases Deemed Successful by the Foreign Ministry
Torture of José Pedro Luis Huerta Galiote

On January 27, 1992, agents of the Judicial Police of Puebla state arbitrarily detained José Pedro Luis Huerta Galiote, whom they accused of raping the son and daughter of the woman with whom he lived. Police held Huerta Galiote incommunicado until January 30, beating him and applying electrical current to his body, causing him to pass out several times. On one occasion when Huerta Galiote was passed out, police inserted a nail into his head.[274] Medical personnel failed to take note of his physical condition.

In a series of indictments beginning in April of 1994, police, medical personnel, and prosecutors were charged with crimes ranging from abuse of authority and battery to crimes against the administration of justice. Several police officers and medical examiners were fired, but no public official was ever sentenced for the torture of Huerta Galiote or for failing to investigate or document the abuse properly. Huerta Galiote is serving a twenty-four-year sentence for rape.[275]

Torture of Omar Carreño Munóz, Luis Alberto Chávez Sarabia, Francisco Javier Reyes Guzmán, and José de Jesús López Bogarin in Sinaloa

On January 20, 1994, four inmates in a Mazatlán, Sinaloa state prison—Omar Carreño Munóz, Luis Alberto Chávez Sarabia, Francisco Javier Reyes Guzmán, and José de Jesús López Bogarin—were taken from their cell after allegedly taunting guards. They were kicked and beaten, then made to lie face down while

---

[273] Office of the Federal Attorney General, "Resultados obtenidos."

[274] National Human Rights Commission, Recommendation 145/92, in *Gaceta* 26 (Mexico City: Comisión Nacional de Derechos Humanos, September 1992), pp. 118-49.

[275] National Human Rights Commission, Coordinating Office for Follow-up on Recommendations (Coordinación de Seguimiento de Recomendaciones), "Recomendación 145/92, 12/Ago/92, Puebla," no date, pp. 4, 14-15. Document sent to Human Rights Watch by Mexico's Foreign Ministry on August 28, 1998.

guards poured pails of cold water and rocks over their backs every five minutes for ninety minutes.[276]

In September 1995, a judge issued arrest warrants for six prison guards for the treatment received by the four prisoners in January of the prior year, but they were accused of abuse of authority and battery, not torture.[277] The CNDH did not provide follow-up information indicating whether the arrest warrants were served.

Torture of Evangelina Arias de Bravo

After Octavio Bravo Arias allegedly stole money from the National Bank of the Army, Air Force and Navy (Banco Nacional del Ejército, Fuerza Aérea y Armada, or Banjército) in 1991, soldiers illegally detained the suspect's mother, Evangelina Arias de Bravo, and forced her to sign a document promising to repay the money they said her son had stolen. She was held in Veracruz state between August 26 and September 3, 1991, and tortured psychologically. They told her that they had her grandchildren in custody and that they were going to force her pregnant daughter to abort her fetus. She signed the document, and Banjército used it to file a successful court case against her in which her house was seized in lieu of payment.[278]

Arias de Bravo filed a complaint with federal prosecutors, who turned the case over to the military, but military investigators failed to investigate thoroughly, lost the file, then closed the case without taking action against the soldiers who had forced her to sign the document.[279]

After the CNDH issued a recommendation, military prosecutors reopened the case and eventually informed the commission that three officers would be charged with torture for their role in the episode. A court eventually reversed the decision to seize Arias de Bravo's home.[280] The CNDH did not provide follow-up information regarding whether the officers were actually indicted.

---

[276] National Human Rights Commission, Recommendation 47/94, in *Gaceta* 46 (Mexico City: Comisión Nacional de Derechos Humanos, May 1994), p. 25.

[277] National Human Rights Commission, Coordinating Office for Follow-up on Recommendations, "Recomendación 047/94, 30/Mar/94, Sinaloa," no date, p. 11. Document sent to Human Rights Watch by Mexico's Foreign Ministry on August 28, 1998.

[278] National Human Rights Commission, Recommendation 114/96, in *Gaceta* 76 (Mexico City: Comisión Nacional de Derechos Humanos, November 1996), pp. 263-64.

[279] Ibid.

[280] National Human Rights Commission, Coordinating Office for Follow-up on Recommendations, "Recomendación 114/96, 15/Nov./96, Federal," no date, p. 8. Document sent to Human Rights Watch by Mexico's Foreign Ministry on August 28, 1998.

Success and Failure in Two Cases Handled by NGOs

Eduardo Garci Crespo

On March 30, 1995, public security police officers killed Eduardo Torres Garci Crespo, a pilot with Mexicana airlines.[281] The officers tried to detain the man in the early morning as he drove through Mexico City's Roma neighborhood. Possibly fearing a robbery, the driver did not heed police calls to stop, so the officers, in four cars, followed Garci Crespo while firing their weapons. The police overtook Garci Crespo at this parents' house, where one of the officers shot him between the eyes.[282]

Following the shooting, the officers repaired to a restaurant until, forty-five minutes later, they received a call related to the murder. They returned to the scene and pretended to investigate, interviewing witnesses and carrying the body to the funeral vehicle.[283]

On April 4, 1995, prosecutors announced that three of the four officers involved in the incident had been arrested; the man believed responsible for shooting Garci Crespo fled but was later captured. For the following year, however, the case progressed little, and the victim's family complained of repeated irregularities, such as the inability of the victim's legal representatives to present their side of the case in court, the refusal of authorities to provide the defense team with a copy of the case file, and, when the file was finally turned over, the fact that 600 of its 1,500 pages were illegible.[284] A tape of the police communications during the chase subsequently disappeared.[285]

On September 2, a judge sentenced each of four former public security police officers to more than thirty-six years in prison for aggravated homicide and abuse of authority.[286] The officer who had fled was found and included in the sentence.

Manuel Manríquez

Manuel Manríquez was detained in Mexico City on June 2, 1990, without an arrest warrant. Subjected to torture, he was forced to confess to a murder. The three courts that ended up hearing his case originally or on appeal accepted his torture-based confession and never questioned the lack of an arrest warrant or the case's other procedural defects, such as the refusal of authorities to let the defendant

---

[281] Miguel Agustín Pro Juárez Human Rights Center, press release, September 3, 1996.
[282] Ibid.
[283] Ibid.
[284] Miguel Agustín Pro Juárez Human Rights Center, press release, no date.
[285] Miguel Agustín Pro Juárez Human Rights Center, press release, September 3, 1996.
[286] Ibid.

attend all hearings related to the trial. According to a judge who eventually heard the torture case, Manríquez

> was taken to the office of the Judicial Police of Iztapalapa Delegation, where they blindfolded him and interrogated him on several occasions, beating him to get him to confess to two homicides. . . . He was beaten day and night. The beatings were on all of his body, and they caused lesions inside his mouth. In addition they burned his testicles with lit cigarettes, and put "Peking chile" up his nose.[287]

Manríquez was found guilty of murder, based in part on his forced confession. The judge who first heard the case cited the confession in the sentence and argued that it was valid even if Manríquez had retracted it. To accept the forced confession, the judge cited the "principle of judicial immediacy," whereby the first confession has more validity than others. On appeal, other courts also used this tortured confession.[288]

Almost five years after the detainee was tortured, Mexico City prosecutors charged two police agents—Fernando Pavón Delgado and José Luis Bañuelos Esquivel—with torture.[289] On November 24, 1995, the agents were arrested. Bañuelos, the alleged perpetrator of the torture, appealed the arrest order on the grounds that a Mexico City prosecutor had filed charges under a federal law, the 1991 Law to Prevent and Punish Torture. On November 27, 1996, a judge ruled in favor of Bañuelos, ordering his immediate release, but noting that a federal prosecutor could still file charges. The federal prosecutor never filed the torture charge against Bañuelos. Six days earlier, a Mexico City judge handed Pavón, who had not appealed the arrest warrant, a two-year sentence.[290] As Bañuelos's superior, Pavón was found guilty of torture for having failed to prevent the abuse by turning the detainee over to prosecutors within the time period allowed by law. Police held Manríquez for five days. The judge allowed Pavón to substitute a fine for prison time.[291]

---

[287] Sentencia, Causa Penal 112/95, Juez Décimo Segundo de Distrito en Material Penal en el Distrito Federal, November 21, 1996, pp. 66-67.

[288] Center for Justice and International Law, legal brief filed before the Inter-American Commission on Human Rights, May 22, 1996, p. 2.

[289] AP 50/ACI/245/94-03 and SC/11982/92. Juzgado Sexagésimo Tercero de lo Penal del Distrito Federal, Causa 175/95.

[290] Resolución, Toca Penal No. 11/96-I, pp. 7-8.

[291] Ibid.

Meanwhile, the torture victim remains in prison. Shortly after the EPR carried out its first public, armed actions in 1996, authorities transferred the detainee to a maximum security prison, arguing that he was a member of the armed group. "There are reasons to believe that these inmates are part of the political organization called PROCUP-PDLP, which supports the activities of the EPR," explained the Ministry of Government.[292] After intense lobbying by human rights lawyers, Manríquez was returned to a Mexico City prison.

Human Rights Commission of the Federal District

Founded in 1994, Mexico City's official Human Rights Commission of the Federal District functions analogously to the CNDH, but its attention is focused exclusively on Mexico City. Its recommendations, which consist of detailed case information and non-binding suggestions for action to be taken by Mexico City officials in human rights cases, have been relatively few in number but forceful and well-documented. They have also been effective in stimulating investigations into serious human rights violations, if not leading to sentences for human rights violators. According to Luis de la Barreda, the commission's president, thirty-four city officials are under criminal investigation for torture at the time of this writing, following commission recommendations.[293] One public servant has been sentenced to nine years and three months in prison, but is not serving his sentence because he fled.[294] De la Barreda also notes that after the commission documented a case of torture that took place in a building housing offices of the city attorney general and judicial police, the prosecutor installed closed-circuit television monitors, in accordance with the commission's recommendation.

The commission highlights one of the key assertions of this report—that with appropriate political will, torture cases can be moved through the system. On March 21, 1995, according to Federal District commission recommendation 12/95, guards at the Men's Preventive Custody-South facility tortured Adrián Marcos Hernández, who had earlier that day refused a request from one of his torturers to relinquish a piece of clothing. According to the guard, the inmate had refused to obey an order to stop using the clothing to block the guards' view of a visiting area. Later that day, the guard entered the man's cell and, along with another prison employee, brought him to a staff doctor. The doctor examined the man and

---

[292] Government Ministry, press release 278/96, September 6, 1996.

[293] Human Rights Commission of the Federal District, "Un refugio probado," April 21, 1998, p. 6.

[294] Human Rights Commission of the Federal District, document given to Human Rights Watch on September 8, 1997.

determined that he had not been beaten. From there, they brought him to a room in another building, where he was beaten by two guards, including the one who had tried to take his clothing. The following day, a fellow inmate brought the victim to a staff doctor, who gave him pills for the pain but refused to fill out a report on the incident. On March 25, a staff doctor finally conducted a medical exam on the victim, but only after the commission intervened.[295]

City prosecutors charged the guards with abuse of authority, not torture, prompting the commission's president to write to the city attorney general to urge that the case be reviewed and that prosecutors charge the guards with torture. "By issuing charges of abuse of authority—which carries a low penalty—and not with torture—which is severely punished, in accord with the seriousness of the criminal act—the opportunity is lost to give the mentioned abuse of authority the just punishment that it deserves."[296] In response, the city broadened the charges to include torture.[297] But even so, the system showed its weakness. When the charge was changed to torture, the prison guards fled.

---

[295] Human Rights Commission of the Federal District, Recommendation 12/95, September 4, 1995, mimeo, pp. 7-8, 15, and 22-23.
[296] Luis de la Barreda Solórzano, letter to then-Attorney General José Antonio González Fernández, January 12, 1996.
[297] Armando Victoria Santamaría, Procuraduría General de Justicia del Distrito Federal, March 28, 1996.

IX. THE ROLE OF THE INTERNATIONAL COMMUNITY

While Mexican government officials and opposition politicians trumpet their disdain for foreign intervention on human rights issues, foreign governments—particularly the United States and members of the European Union—are increasingly active in monitoring and commenting on Mexico's human rights abuses, especially those related to the troubled southern state of Chiapas. Similarly, the human rights bodies of international organizations such as the United Nations and the Organization of American States are playing a greater role in Mexico now than at any time in the past.

Raising the sovereignty flag, however, is a politically expedient method for Mexico to deflect criticism, sidetrack debate, and raise the political stakes for countries that do speak out on the country's human rights record. On numerous occasions in 1998, for instance, Mexican authorities successfully deflected foreign concern over human rights problems by engaging in political debates on sovereignty, thereby eliminating all discussion of the substance of the underlying human rights issues. Such was the case when, during a U.S. Senate hearing on June 16, 1998, Secretary of State Madeleine Albright answered a query from Sen. Patrick Leahy by replying that Mexico was aware of U.S. concerns about Chiapas and noting that the U.S. was "pressing" Mexico for a peaceful solution. A diplomatic row ensued, covered intensely in the Mexican press, over whether the secretary meant to say the United States was pressuring Mexico or was simply voicing concern. Absent from the debate was any focus on the human rights violations that had occurred in Chiapas. Similarly, the government's expulsion of foreign monitors in Chiapas in April 1998 shifted the debate from what the foreigners had observed to the fact that they had done so.

The Mexican government has strongly criticized Human Rights Watch for calling on foreign governments to express public and private concern about human rights conditions in Mexico. In April 1997, on the day that Human Rights Watch published *Implausible Deniability: State Responsibility for Rural Violence in Mexico*, the Mexican Foreign Ministry responded to what it described as the "curious" timing of the report, since President Bill Clinton planned to visit Mexico two weeks later:

> Moreover, in the press release it issued today, Human Rights Watch/Americas suggests that the visiting head of state underscore during his visit the importance of strengthening the rule of law in the country and the need to end impunity for political violence. This organization seems to forget that Mexico is a sovereign country and,

therefore, that it does not receive instructions from any foreign government at all.[298]

A yawning gap exists, however, between receiving orders from abroad and acknowledging criticism or even suggestions on issues related to internationally recognized human rights standards. It is the province of all people and governments to support the protection and promotion of human rights in any country, and Mexico's compliance or failure to comply with international human rights standards is a matter of public interest both within and outside Mexico's borders. The Universal Declaration of Human Rights, a cornerstone of international human rights standards, proclaims, ". . . every individual and every organ of society, keeping this Declaration constantly in mind, shall strive by teaching and education to promote respect for these rights and freedoms and by progressive measures, national and international, to secure their universal and effective recognition and observance. . . ."[299] Raising human rights concerns abroad becomes even more necessary when countries increasingly integrate their economies, coordinate cross-border initiatives such as anti-narcotics measures, and agree to cross-border training of military personnel, as have Mexico and the United States. Indeed, Human Rights Watch believes that these realities confer on the United States the responsibility to encourage greater respect for human rights in Mexico, and on Mexico to promote greater respect for human rights in the United States. Similarly, by signing a trade, political, and cooperation agreement with the European Union, Mexico has expressly committed itself to cross-border scrutiny of its human rights practices.

United States Human Rights Policy Toward Mexico
Policies and assistance

The State Department is well aware of the serious human rights violations that take place in Mexico. The most recent *Country Reports on Human Rights Practices* noted,

> Major abuses included extrajudicial killings, disappearances, torture, illegal arrests, arbitrary detentions, poor prison conditions, lengthy

---

[298] Foreign Ministry, press release 134, April 29, 1997. Translation by Human Rights Watch.

[299] The Universal Declaration of Human Rights was adopted and proclaimed by United Nations General Assembly resolution 217 A(III) on December 10, 1948.

pretrial detention, lack of due process, corruption and inefficiency in the judiciary, illegal searches, violence against women, discrimination against women and indigenous persons, some limits on worker rights, and extensive child labor in agriculture and in the informal economy.[300]

The State Department has also held important meetings with Mexican human rights organizations and carried out human rights fact-finding missions headed by State Department officials from Washington, D.C. These efforts send a pro-human rights message to Mexican government officials and human rights monitors alike. When it comes to establishing U.S. policy toward Mexico, however, human rights occupies a place on the bilateral agenda far behind trade, immigration, and drugs. The State Department treads very lightly with respect to human rights in Mexico, failing to take public positions on key human rights issues, such as the arbitrary expulsion of U.S. citizens from Mexico. When two U.S. citizens were expelled in April 1998, U.S. officials only raised with their Mexican counterparts concern over whether U.S. embassy personnel had been adequately notified. No concern was raised over the arbitrary expulsion itself.

At the same time, the United States armed forces are increasingly training Mexican soldiers and providing assistance to Mexican civilian agencies involved in counternarcotics initiatives. Mexico receives more International Military Education and Training (IMET) funding than any other Latin American or Caribbean country, at an estimated cost of U.S. $1 million for 190 Mexican trainees in 1998, with a similar amount requested for 1999. Another $5 million is expected to be spent during 1998 on International Narcotics Control initiatives in Mexico; $8 million has been requested for the following year. These funds will be disbursed to the PGR, the Northern Border Response Team (a joint civilian-military task force), and other Mexican agencies.

The Pentagon also spent more than $28 million training Mexicans in 1997, and it is expected to spend slightly more than $20 million for training in 1998. These funds—known as Section 1004, after its location in the 1991 Defense Authorization Act—are for counternarcotics initiatives only, including U.S. military training of foreign police forces. However, the Defense Department is not required to break down its spending by category. Under this program, the United States trained 829 Mexicans, many of them from Mobile Air Special Forces Groups (Grupos Aeromóviles de Fuerzas Especiales, GAFE).

---

[300] U.S. Department of State, *Country Reports on Human Rights Practices for 1997* (Washington, DC: U.S. Government Printing Office, February 1998), pp. 570-71.

The United States has also delivered aircraft and helicopters to Mexico under the president's Emergency Drawdown Authority (EDA). In 1996 and 1997, the United States transferred fifty-three UJ-1H helicopters and three C-26 aircraft. Another twenty helicopters were transferred through the Excess Defense Articles (EDA) program. End-use monitoring of these helicopters has been weak, according to the General Accounting Office (GAO). The U.S. embassy in Mexico City was found to have kept incomplete records of the use of the helicopters, while the U.S. military's ability to provide adequate oversight was limited by the end-use monitoring agreement itself.[301]

United States Agency for International Development (USAID) programs in Mexico, valued at $15 million for fiscal year 1998 and $13 million for 1999, included a judicial exchange initiative focused on bringing together U.S. and Mexican judges. The programs do not include an explicit human rights focus.

Human rights concerns with U.S. assistance to Mexico

The United States has encouraged Mexico's military to play a larger role in counternarcotics efforts. As the United States encourages Mexico's military to become further involved in civilian-related law enforcement activities, the U.S. government has not enunciated a medium- or long-term plan to strengthen civilian institutions so that Mexico's army will not indefinitely need to play the role it has currently assumed, and the United States has not made Mexico's development of such a plan a condition of U.S. training. United States support of Mexico's army in these roles may undermine the civilian institutions that should undergird any democratic society.

Although training is ostensibly for anti-narcotics matters, the reality in Mexico is that troops engaged in fighting the production or traffic of illegal drugs are likely to be called to engage in counterinsurgency as well. Guerrero state, for instance, produces drugs and has a guerrilla presence; soldiers working on one issue cannot realistically be expected not to engage in the other.

At the same time, serious human rights violations have been documented in U.S.-supported anti-drug operations, as indicated by the Hodoyán and Soto Miller cases, analyzed in the chapter on "disappearances," and in cases involving U.S.-trained soldiers. The United States became complicit in the Hodoyán "disappearance" by failing to aid the U.S. citizen who was encountered in military

---

[301] Adam Isacson and Joy Olson, *Just the Facts: A Civilian's Guide to U.S. Defense and Security Assistance to Latin America and the Caribbean* (Washington, DC: Latin America Working Group, 1998), p. 60.

custody. Apparently more interested in pumping the man for information on drug trafficking, U.S. officials did nothing to assist the victim. In Jalisco state, U.S.-trained Mexican soldiers participated in the arbitrary detention and torture of some twenty people on December 14 and 15, 1997, one of whom was killed.[302] The soldiers planned the attack in advance, apparently after someone stole one of their weapons, and the victims were brought to and tortured at the military base.[303] According to Mexico's *La Jornada* newspaper, the Pentagon confirmed that six of the soldiers had been trained under the Pentagon's Section 1004 program.[304] The soldiers have been arrested but are facing trial in military, not civilian, court.[305] "The United States played no role in monitoring these soldiers after training," a State Department official told Human Rights Watch. "That is the policy because it is not practical to follow each and every one of them. At the same time, the fact is that the Mexican government would never stand for it."[306]

If the United States is to persist in training Mexican law-enforcement agents, it cannot continue to tread lightly with regard to human rights issues simply because the Mexican government would reject it. The responsibility engendered by U.S. training, funding, and equipping of Mexican officials makes promoting and protecting human rights there a necessity, not an option.

The European Union

On December 8, 1997, Mexico and the European Union signed an economic partnership, political coordination, and cooperation agreement, bringing to a close negotiations that included intense scrutiny of Mexico's human rights record.[307] In June of the previous year, Mexico and the European Commission, responsible for negotiating with non-E.U. states, had agreed on terms for the pact, but the union's Council of Ministers rejected the deal on the grounds that Mexico had excised the

---

[302] Human Rights Watch telephone interview, María Guadalupe Morfín, president, Jalisco State Human Rights Commission, August 5, 1998.

[303] Ibid.

[304] Jim Cason and David Brooks, "Violaron derechos humanos en Jalisco militares entrenados en EU," *La Jornada*, June 28, 1998.

[305] Human Rights Watch telephone interview, María Guadalupe Morfín.

[306] Human Rights Watch interview, August 5, 1998.

[307] Mexico and the European Union will begin negotiations on trade issues in late 1998.

standard human rights and democracy clause from the agreement.[308] Mexico had reportedly objected to the clause's inclusion of domestic policies within the realm of issues open to evaluation by the Europeans. Eventually, Mexico relented, and the clause was included in the agreement signed in December.

As part of the accord signed in December, Mexico and the E.U. agreed to an interim agreement regulating trade negotiations, which entered into force on July 1, 1998. Before it became effective, members of the European Parliament issued recommendations with regard to the accord. The committees on foreign economic affairs, foreign affairs, security and defense policy, and cooperation and development urged the Council of Ministers to ensure that funds for democracy and human rights projects would come available at the same time that the agreement entered into force. The latter two committees also urged the Council of Ministers to take steps to ensure that during the annual meetings of the Joint Committee, which will review the implementation of the accord, explicit attention be paid to human rights issues. In order for either of these suggestions to come to fruition, however, either the Europeans or the Mexicans will have to insist on them.

Funding for democracy and human rights projects and an annual review of Mexico's human rights practices could play an important role in promoting human rights in Mexico. Given that the agreement is conditioned upon respect for human rights and democratic principles, it could serve to press Mexico for important improvements, either expressly or tacitly.

The European Union should build on the solid human rights foundation it has developed with Mexico to ensure that the new economic partnership, political coordination, and cooperation agreement becomes an instrument through which the effective protection of human rights is encouraged in Mexico. The various components of the E.U. should work rapidly to ensure that funds for democracy and human rights projects in Mexico become available as soon as possible; a review of human rights conditions in Mexico takes place as part of any annual evaluation of the functioning of the accord; written reports and oral testimonies on human rights are solicited from governmental and nongovernmental sources as part of the annual review process; and the permanent mission of the European Commission in Mexico City is staffed with at least one full-time human rights monitor who is provided the resources necessary to report exhaustively on human rights conditions there.

---

[308] The clause reads, "Respect for democratic principles and fundamental human rights, proclaimed by the Universal Declaration of Human Rights, underpins the domestic and external policies of both Parties and constitutes an essential element of this Agreement."

The United Nations and the Organization of American States

After years of requesting permission to conduct an official mission to Mexico, U.N. Special Rapporteur on Torture Nigel Rodley conducted research in Mexico in August 1997. He released a detailed report in January 1998, concluding, "Torture and analogous mistreatment occur with frequency in many parts of Mexico, although the information received by the Special Rapporteur does not permit the conclusion that it is a systematic practice in all parts of the country."[309] The report made detailed recommendations.

The special rapporteur's scrutiny was followed in June 1998 by interest in Chiapas by U.N. High Commissioner for Human Rights Mary Robinson, who expressed concern about human rights violations there. She announced that her office stood ready to provide technical assistance if it was requested by the Mexican government. Although she was strongly rebuffed by the government at the outset, Mexican authorities hinted in early August, when Secretary-General Kofi Annan visited Mexico, that she might be permitted to visit Chiapas. According to the office of the high commissioner for human rights, in mid-August the Mexican government, through its mission at the United Nations in Geneva, requested technical assistance from the office of the high commissioner. "The request was general and could serve as the basis for discussion with the Mexican government about what the assistance might consist of," the office told Human Rights Watch.[310] Despite the fact that the U.N. Human Rights Committee confirmed the Mexican request for assistance, Mexico's Foreign Ministry denied that a request had been made.

The details of the technical human rights assistance have yet to be ironed out between the high commissioner and Mexican government. If the Mexican government were to permit it, the commission could send an evaluation team to conduct research on ways in which the Mexican government could improve its human rights record, and could make public its report and recommendations.

Both the secretary-general and high commissioner for human rights have met with Mexican human rights organizations, the former during his trip to Mexico and the latter in Geneva. These meetings served both as a positive message of support for the human rights community and as an important opportunity for the United Nations officials to receive first-hand information about human rights violations in Mexico.

---

[309] Inter-American Commission on Human Rights, "Report on the Situation of Human Rights in Mexico," para. 78.

[310] Human Rights Watch telephone interview, September 2, 1998.

The Inter-American Commission on Human Rights, an organ of the Organization of American States, is also playing an increasingly active role in Mexico. The September 1998 commission report on Mexico provided important analysis of the overall human rights situation in Mexico. The commission has also investigated multiple individual cases of human rights violations in Mexico and pushed Mexican authorities to resolve the problems found.

Taken together, the U.N. and the OAS have worked to legitimate the cause of international attention to human rights violations in Mexico, although the Mexican government has not openly accepted their recommendations. Rather, the international attention appears to be considered by authorities as one more political inconvenience among others to be weathered.

The Organization of American States and the United Nations should persist in their efforts to investigate human rights conditions in Mexico and to publish detailed reports and recommendations on their findings. In particular, the Inter-American Commission on Human Rights should maintain its investigations into individual cases and should use its broad experience on Mexico to promote human rights reforms there. The United Nations should continue to make known its availability to assist the Mexican government through the office of the high commissioner for human rights.

HV 6322.3 .M6 897 1995

Systemic injustice

DATE DUE

MAY 1 2 2006			

Demco, Inc. 38-293